A READER IN ISSUES IN INTERNATIONAL TRADE

TABLE OF CONTENTS

*** BOOK PRINTED BY TIGERPRESS, NORTHAMPTON, MASS.**
ISBN: 978-0615398365

Price: $15.99 plus S&H

PREFACE

This is a *reader* about international trade. It is not meant to be a traditional text or an exhaustive review of the entire topic. Rather, it has been prepared by experts in their fields of international finance, international marketing and management, and international law, business ethics and organizations in order to give its readers valuable insights into this topic.

The reader contains an important "set up" piece that will outline the major components of and trends in international trade—especially as they relate to Foreign Direct Investment and economic development; takes a look at the international trading system from the creation of the GATT in 1945 through the coming into force of the WTO; describes the dispute resolution mechanism under the WTO; and outlines some of the major tariff and nontariff barriers that serve as impediments to a further development and opening of international trade.

In addition, the reader provides insights into various current issues in international trade, including dumping and subsidization, issues relating to compulsory licensing of intellectual property rights, a discussion of products liability issues concerning ever-growing imports from China, a discussion of the interconnection of the environment and the WTO with appurtenant ethical considerations and concludes with an essay on "current topics" of particular interest.

As a supplement to a course textbook or to classroom lectures, the reader has been carefully prepared to bring rich context to the areas of finance, law, business ethics, marketing and management that make up the core foundational elements of the regime of international trading. This volume reflects the various research methodologies of each of the authors. A comprehensive bibliography has been provided at the conclusion of the articles in social-science format in order to assist further research and investigation.

Authors Dr. Héctor Lozada and Dr. Yeomin Yoon of the Stillman School of Business at Seton Hall University are long-time researchers into their fields and have served for many years as consultants to the United Nations Institute on Teaching and Research, facilitating workshops in international trade, development, and foreign direct investment at the United Nations headquarters in New York City and in Hiroshima, Japan. Dr. Lozada is the former Director of the Institute for International Business at Seton Hall University as well. Dr. Mark Blodgett is Director of the Center for Global Business, Ethics and Law at Suffolk University. The editor, a Professor of Legal Studies at Seton Hall University, has joined the other authors in many of the activities previously mentioned. He currently teaches International Trade Regulation at Rutgers University School of Law, Newark and Camden campuses, and is a specialist in transition economies where issues relating to international trade are paramount in assuring the long-range success of transformation strategies. Dr.

Robert McGee is a prolific researcher and teaches accounting at Florida International University. We are also joined by Frank Giarratano, Dan Jenkins and Aaron Gordon, outstanding students from the MBA program at the Stillman School of Business at Seton Hall University who provided basic research for Chapters two and three.

We hope that this reader will serve as a valuable and practical resource for both faculty and students involved in careful study of core issues relating to the environment and practices of international trade.

We wish to acknowledge the following journal publications where the basic research has previously appeared:

Compulsory Licensing: A Major IP Issue in International Business Today?
European Journal of Social Sciences
Vol. 11, Issue 3, pp. 370-377 (Nov. 2009)

Understanding and Negotiating the Products Liability Pitfalls of Outsourcing to China: Systemic Failures or Isolated Product Defects?
International Bulletin of Business Administration (ISSN: 145-243X)
Issue 6, pp. 28-39 (Fall 2009)

The Environment and Trade Agreements: Should the WTO Become More Actively Involved?
Hastings International and Comparative Law Review
Vol. 33, pp. 1-19 (Winter 2010)

CHAPTER 1

A PRIMER ON ISSUES IN INTERNATIONAL TRADE

"International trade involves the purchase, sale or exchange (barter transactions) of goods and services across national borders."

Richard J. Hunter, Jr.
And
Héctor R. Lozada

1. Introduction: Some Definitional Considerations

As an important part of an understanding of international trade, some definitions might be in order. The *capital account* is an account that records transactions involving the purchase or sale of tangible assets. The *current account* is the account that records transactions involving the import and export of goods and services, income receipts on assets abroad, and income payments on foreign assets inside the country. The *merchandise account* includes imports and exports of tangible goods. The *services account* includes exports and imports of services such as tourism, consulting, and banking and financial services.

The *current account surplus* occurs when a country exports more goods and services than it imports. This situation results in what is traditionally termed as a *trade surplus*. A *current account deficit* occurs when a country imports more than it exports, traditionally termed a *trade deficit*.

These definitions lay a foundation for some of the core aspects of international trade.

The Context

2009 was anything but a banner year for international or global trade—or for the international economy.[1] The World Bank reported that the volume of international trade actually fell by 14.4 percent. Bernard Hoekman, Director of the World Bank's trade group, reported that the dismal showing in international trade reflected the general position of the world economy which experienced a "distinct slowdown" in the pace of expected recovery towards the end of 2009. In fact, preliminary figures for November 2009 indicated an expansion of world trade by a paltry 1.1 percent, less than the small increase recorded for October of 1.4 percent, and far less than the encouraging 5.4 percent rise in September 2009.

---

[1] Trade data in the introduction has been adapted from "Fading trading," *The Economist*, Jan. 30, 2010, p. 85.

The *Economist* explained that the expected resurgence in international trade may have literally fizzled because the growth in the third quarter of 2009 had been artificially buoyed by the rebuilding of business inventories, which had been slashed during the most desperate period of the world economic crisis experienced in 2009.

A second explanation may be found in exploring the sources of global demand, which has come mainly from developing and emerging markets. In fact, the ten countries whose foreign sales grew fastest in the three month period to October 2009 were all developing and emerging markets—including several Eastern European nations, plus Indonesia, and South Africa. The fastest growing representative developed nation was Australia, which exported nearly a quarter of its products to China and India. On the other side of the equation, none of the ten countries whose imports grew most rapidly were emerging markets. China leads the pack—perhaps somewhat artificially as a result of its program of stimulus spending.

China's share of world imports has grown from around 10 percent at the mid-point of 2008 to over 12 percent in 2009. Germany's exports grew by a healthy 3.3 percent in the three month period to September 2009. Demand in China has also boosted exports from Japan which grew by 12.1 percent in the year to December 2009. China has recently replaced America as Japan's biggest market.

Many of the decidedly negative consequences of the international economy may be alleviated by an expected rise in GDP for developed countries by 2.1% in 2010 and 2.4% in 2011. Overall, the world economy is expected to grow by a respectable 3.9% in 2010. How the renewed growth in the international economy will impact on international trade is yet to be determined.

While international trade is in itself a very important component of international economic growth and development, it certainly plays an integral role in terms of its impact on foreign direct investment or FDI. The confluence of international trade and investment is striking.

The intersection of international trade and foreign direct investment may also be reflected in the precipitous drop in the flows of foreign direct investment by 39% in 2009 to just over $1.7 trillion in 2008. The UN Conference on Trade and Development reported that all kinds of investment—equity capital, reinvested earnings, and intra company loans—were greatly affected by the economic downturn experienced in 2009. Rich or "develop" countries saw FDI inflows drop by 41%. FDI into developing countries fell by more than one-third. Professor George Yipp notes that among the most important ways a host government negatively impacts the process of globalization and FDI inflows are in fact some of the core issues involving international trade. He lists them as import tariffs and quotas, nontariff barriers, export subsidies, local content requirements, currency and capital flow restrictions, ownership restrictions, and requirements on technology transfers.[2]

---

[2] George S. Yip, *Total Global Strategy II* (2003), p. 50.

This introduction to international trade is designed to assist the reader to gain an overall picture of international trade as it has developed since World War II. Topical coverage includes a discussion of the post-War War II trading system known as the GATT, the creation of the WTO in 1995, mechanisms created for settling trade disputes, and a brief introduction into two major areas of contention—dumping and illegal subsidization.

2. The Global Trading System: A Brief Overview and History

The global trading system is fraught with many pitfalls and dangers.[3] The following are some of the main barriers to free trade; many of the examples are taken from Chinese trade practices:[4]

---

3. The GATT system is comprised of specific country groups, organized by region:

North America: Canada, United States of America, and territories in North America.

Latin America: Antigua and Barbuda, Argentina, Bahamas, Barbados, Belize, Bolivia, Brazil, Chile, Colombia, Costa Rica, Cuba, Dominica, Dominican Republic, Ecuador, El Salvador, Grenada, Guatemala, Guyana, Haiti, Honduras, Jamaica, Mexico, Netherlands Antilles, Nicaragua, Panama, Paraguay, Peru, Saint Kitts and Nevis, Saint Lucia, Saint Vincent and the Grenadines, Suriname, Trinidad and Tobago, Uruguay, Venezuela and other countries and territories in Latin America.

Western Europe: Austria, Belgium, Denmark, Finland, France, Germany, Greece, Iceland, Ireland, Italy, Liechtenstein, Luxembourg, Malta, Netherlands, Norway, Portugal, Spain, Sweden, Switzerland, Turkey, United Kingdom, Bosnia and Herzegovina, Croatia, former Yugoslav Republic of Macedonia, Slovenia, Yugoslavia (the last five countries mentioned comprise the former Yugoslavia), and territories in Western Europe.

Central and Eastern Europe, the Baltic States and the Commonwealth of Independent States (transition economies), of which *Central and Eastern Europe*: Albania, Bulgaria, Czech Republic, Hungary, Poland, Romania and the Slovak Republic; *the Baltic States*: Estonia, Latvia and Lithuania; and *the Commonwealth of Independent States (CIS)*: Armenia, Azerbaijan, Belarus, Georgia, Kazakhstan, Kyrgyz Republic, Republic of Moldova, Russian Federation, Tajikistan, Turkmenistan, Ukraine and Uzbekistan. The grouping *former USSR* refers to the Baltic States and the CIS.

Africa, of which *North Africa*: Algeria, Egypt, Libyan Arab Jamahiriya, Morocco and Tunisia; and *Sub-Saharan Africa* comprising: *Western Africa*: Benin, Burkina Faso, Cape Verde, Côte d'Ivoire, Gambia, Ghana, Guinea, Guinea-Bissau, Liberia, Mali, Mauritania, Niger, Nigeria, Senegal, Sierra Leone and Togo; *Central Africa*: Burundi, Cameroon, Central African Republic, Chad, Congo, Democratic Republic of the Congo, Equatorial Guinea, Gabon, Rwanda, and Sao Tome and Principe; *Eastern Africa*: Comoros, Djibouti, Eritrea, Ethiopia, Kenya, Madagascar, Mauritius, Seychelles, Somalia, Sudan, United Republic of Tanzania and Uganda; and *Southern Africa:* Angola, Botswana, Lesotho, Malawi, Mozambique, Namibia, South Africa, Swaziland, Zambia, Zimbabwe and territories in Africa.

The Middle East: Bahrain, Cyprus, Iraq, Islamic Republic of Iran, Israel, Jordan, Kuwait, Lebanon, Oman, Qatar, Saudi Arabia, Syrian Arab Republic, United Arab Emirates, Yemen and other countries and territories in the Middle East.

Asia, of which *West Asia*: Afghanistan, Bangladesh, Bhutan, India, Maldives, Nepal, Pakistan and Sri Lanka; and *East Asia (including Oceania)*: Australia; Brunei Darussalam; Cambodia; China; Fiji; Hong Kong Special

a. High tariffs;
b. Pervasive non-tariff barriers (quotas, licenses, registration requirements, "buy local" legislation, restrictive technical, labeling,[5] and sanitary standards, and embargoes);
c. Restrictive trading rights;
d. Restrictive distribution rights;
e. Investment restrictions;
f. Voluntary export restraints.[6]

The General Agreement on Tariffs and Trade (GATT) was a multilateral treaty that was formed in 1947 by 23 nations. GATT came into force in January 1948. At that time, these 23 countries accounted for 80% of the world's trade. Recall that Western Europe was still struggling to recover from the ravages of World War II; Japan was under the authority of the United States; and colonialism reigned supreme in many nations of Africa, South-East Asia, and other parts of the world. GATT negotiations were conducted in what were termed eight separate "*Rounds*." The purpose of the GATT was to promote free trade by reducing both tariff and non-tariff barriers to international trade.[7] The GATT was devised to be a temporary regime—yet it lasted for nearly 50 years before it was replaced by the WTO in 1995.

GATT Rounds

A trade round involves a cycle of multilateral trade negotiations conducted under the authority of GATT, normally culminating in simultaneous trade agreements among participating countries to reduce tariff and non-tariff barriers to trade. Eight separate "Rounds" have been completed thus far: Geneva, 1947-48; Annecy, France, 1949;

Administrative Region of China (Hong Kong, China); Indonesia; Japan; Kiribati; Lao People's Democratic Republic; Macau, China; Malaysia; Mongolia; Myanmar; New Zealand; Papua New Guinea; Philippines; Republic of Korea; Samoa; Separate Customs Territory of Taiwan, Penghu, Kinmen and Matsu (Taipei, Chinese); Singapore; Solomon Islands; Thailand; Tonga; Tuvalu; Vanuatu; Viet Nam and other countries and territories in Asia and the Pacific.

4 For a discussion of the various concerns raised over China's international trade regime, see Raj Bhala, "The Development of the GATT-WTO," in *International Trade Law: Theory and Practice* (2d ed., 2000), pp. 154-155. Professor Bhala provides a comprehensive review of Chinese accession negotiations to the WTO on pp. 155-183.

5 For example, designers like Ferragamo, Gucci, and Versace are required to include the phrase "*Made in China*" on the label of garments that contain silk from China. *See* Blaise J. Bergiel & Erich B. Bergiel, "Country-of-Origin as a Surrogate Indicator" Implications/Strategies," *Global Competitiveness*, Vol. 7 (1999), p. 187.

6 For a comprehensive list of trade barriers, see Mark Magnier, "Blockades to Food Exports Hide Behind Invisible Shields," *The Journal of Commerce*, Vol. 18 (1999), p. 5A.

7 *See generally* Department of the Treasury, "Harmonized Trade Schedule of the United States Code of Federal Regulations No. 19, Customs Duties, Importing into the United States" (1991).

Torquay, England, 1950-51; Geneva, 1956; Geneva, 1960-62 (the Dillon Round); Geneva, 1963-67 (the Kennedy Round); Geneva, 1973-79 (the Tokyo Round); and Geneva, 1986-1993 (the "Uruguay Round").[8] There is a current series of negotiations, the "Doha Round," that have been marked by sharp disagreement between developing and developed nations. The most important of the negotiations conducted under the aegis of the GATT have included:

Dillon Round: The trade negotiations that took place from 1960 to 1962 were named after C. Douglas Dillon, then the U.S. under secretary of state, who had publicly proposed the negotiations. This Round involved 45 countries and about 4,400 tariff concessions covering $4.9 billion of trade.

Kennedy Round: This is popular name for the sixth and at that time the most ambitious Round of trade negotiations. The Kennedy Round, which lasted from 1963 to 1967, produced concrete agreements reducing prevailing tariff levels maintained by developed countries on industrial products by about one-third, produced an historic *Antidumping Code*,[9] and a rather short-lived International Wheat Agreement which was intended to stabilize world wheat prices—an agreement which was subsequently withdrawn and never implemented. The Kennedy Round involved 48 countries and $40 billion in international trade.[10]

Tokyo Round: The Tokyo Round of multilateral trade negotiations was formally initiated by the 1973 Tokyo Declaration. It was by far the most comprehensive effort up to that time to eliminate, reduce or control some of the most pervasive non-tariff barriers that restricted non-agricultural trade. The Tokyo Round was especially important because it negotiated several codes of conduct designed to curtail the use of non-tariff barriers as instruments of trade protection. The Tokyo Round resulted in the *Tokyo Round Antidumping Code*. Like its predecessor, the Tokyo Round Antidumping Code contained rules and procedures concerning the content of antidumping regulations. An important feature of the 1979 Code was a requirement that antidumping investigations be reported, and a semi-annual report on cases be submitted to the GATT Secretariat. More countries (102) participated in these negotiations than in any previous Round. The Round involved $300 billion in trade. Most notably, more than 20 developing countries that were not GATT members and several countries of Eastern Europe with very different economic

---

[8] John Daniels, Lee H. Radebaugh & Daniel Sullivan, "Theories and Institutions: Trade and Investment," in *International Business* (2007), p. 270. *See also* Robert Gilpin, *The Political Economy of International Relations* (1987), p. 192.

[9] As result, during the Kennedy Round, the GATT Antidumping Code of 1967 was established. Its three main functions were: (1) to clarify and elaborate on the broad concepts found in Article VI of the GATT; (2) to supplement Article VI by establishing appropriate procedural requirements for antidumping investigations; and (3) to bring all GATT signatory countries into conformity with Article VI. *See* House Committee on Ways and Means, 104th Cong., 1st Sess., *Overview and Compilation of U.S. Trade Statutes* (June 25, 1997), p. 66.

[10] *See* Kenneth W. Dam, *The GATT* (1970), pp. 68-73, 76-77.

systems were active participants. The Tokyo Round was carried out in Geneva and concluded there in 1979.[11]

Uruguay Round: The Uruguay Round, concluded in Geneva in December 1993, was the latest series of concluded multilateral trade negotiations aimed at revising, updating and expanding the coverage of the GATT. The Uruguay Round was formally launched in September 1986 at the GATT Ministerial in Punta del Este, Uruguay. The negotiations concentrated once again on the elimination of tariff and non-tariff barriers to trade and on the development of clear, transparent, and enforceable international trading rules. The provisions of the Uruguay Round agreement especially considered the unique perspective of developing countries struggling to establish regimes of international trade. The final agreement accorded more time to developing countries than to industrialized countries in order to come into compliance with trading rules. The category of least developed countries (LDCs) were accorded even more time or exempted altogether from some of the provisions of the agreement.[12] The Uruguay Round involved 118 countries and $3.7 trillion in trade.

The following are the main points of the Uruguay Round agreement:

- **Tariffs**: GATT member countries agreed to cut their import tariffs by a 36-percent average.
- **Textiles**: Countries agreed to end the 20-year-old system of import quotas on textiles and apparel by 2005; tariff quotas would be converted into tariffs, which would then be subjected to further reductions over time.
- **Agriculture**: Countries agreed to scale back direct export subsidies by 36 percent below rates in place between 1986 and 1990, by 2001; countries also agreed to reduce the quantity of subsidized commodities exported. They also agreed to convert quotas, import licenses, and other import limits into tariffs that would be gradually reduced.
- **Services**: For the first time, countries agreed to create basic rules so that services providers were afforded the same treatment in host countries as in their home markets.
- **Intellectual Property**: As an important concession to developed countries, negotiators agreed to protect and enforce patent rights, trademarks, and copyrights, and to limit the trade of counterfeited creative works and inventions.

---

[11] *See* Kenneth W. Dam, *The GATT* (1970), pp. 72-73; Robert Gilpin, *The Political Economy of International Trade Relations* (1987), pp. 196-197.

[12] Least-developed countries include: Afghanistan, Angola, Bangladesh, Benin, Bhutan, Burkina Faso, Burundi, Cambodia, Cape Verde, Central African Republic, Chad, Comoros, Democratic Republic of the Congo, Djibouti, Equatorial Guinea, Eritrea, Ethiopia, Gambia, Guinea, Guinea-Bissau, Haiti, Kiribati, Lao People's Democratic Republic, Lesotho, Liberia, Madagascar, Malawi, Maldives, Mali, Mauritania, Mozambique, Myanmar, Nepal, Niger, Rwanda, Samoa, Sao Tome and Principe, Senegal, Sierra Leone, Solomon Islands, Somalia, Sudan, Togo, Tuvalu, Uganda, United Republic of Tanzania, Vanuatu, Yemen and Zambia.

Article 3 of the TRIPS Agreement[13] mandates national treatment for intellectual property protection. Article 4 creates a "Most Favored Nation" obligation for such protection.[14]

- **Investments**: Concerning foreign direct investment or FDI, countries agreed to eliminate investment measures that limit or force certain types of investments, for example, the "golden share"; to offer full "national treatment" to foreign investors; and to eliminate quotas on investments and other financial restraints.
- **Subsidies**: Countries agreed to create rules concerning the legality of subsidies by defining three classes of subsidization: *prohibited, actionable, and non-actionable subsidies.*
- **Dumping**: Countries agreed to create more detailed rules governing the ability of GATT members to take action against the importation of a product sold at an unfairly discounted export price, i.e., to attack the problem known as "dumping."
- **Safeguards**: Countries agreed to strengthen rules concerning "temporary import limits" created to protect domestic industries from surges of fairly-traded imports (i.e., safeguards). Members agreed not to maintain safeguard protections for more than eight years, and to prohibit "gray area measures"—in essence, voluntary export restraints and other informal agreements to curtail fairly traded imports.
- **Institutional Structure**: Perhaps most importantly, members agreed to create a **World Trade Organization**, which would be a permanent international organization representing all of the major economic classifications of nations (developed, developing, least developed), that would replace the GATT with a stronger, permanent institution.
- **Dispute Resolution**: The GATT was not originally intended to be an international organization, but was rather intended to be a *traditional multilateral treaty* designed to function under the *International Trade Organization* (ITO). However, the ITO never came into being. It would be fair to conclude that by default, the GATT became the governing body for settling international trade disputes. There was one major problem: the GATT had no independent enforcement mechanism. It had to rely on "moral suasion," or the good will of member countries. The GATT achieved major progress in increasing the nature and volume of world trade. In the interim period, members agreed to strengthen GATT's dispute resolution rules by allowing countries to block findings by GATT expert panels, but only if all members opposed the finding.[15]

---

[13] The TRIPS Agreement is Annex 1C of the *Marrakesh Agreement Establishing the World Trade Organization*, signed in Marrakesh, Morocco on 15 April 1994.

[14] *See* House of Representatives [Uruguay Round Trade Agreement], *Statement of Administrative Action, Agreement on Trade-Related Aspects of Intellectual Property Rights*, H.R. Doc. No. 316, 103d Cong., 2d Sess., Vol. 1 (Sept. 27, 1994), pp. 981-990.

[15] A 1994 Congressional act established the relationship between the Uruguay Round agreements and U.S. law. *See* House of Representatives [Uruguay Round Trade Agreement], *Statement of Administrative Action, Agreement Establishing the World Trade Organization*, H.R. Doc. No. 316, 103d Cong., 2d Sess., Vol. 1 (Sept. 27, 1994), pp. 669-678.

Doha Round

The Doha Development Round or Doha Development Agenda (DDA) is the current trade-negotiation round under the authority of the World Trade Organization (WTO), which commenced in November 2001. As of 2010, talks remained stalled over a divide on several issues including agriculture, industrial tariffs, non-tariff barriers, services, and trade remedies. The most significant differences lie between developed nations led by the European Union (EU), the United States, and Japan and the major developing countries represented mainly by India, Brazil, China, and South Africa. Considerable contention also existed between the EU and the United States over the United States' maintenance of agricultural subsidies—seen to operate effectively as a trade barrier against agricultural imports from the European Union.

The Doha Round began with a ministerial-level meeting in Doha, Qatar in 2001. Subsequent ministerial meetings took place in Cancún, Mexico (2003),[16] and Hong Kong (2005). Related negotiations took place in Geneva, Switzerland (2004, 2006, 2008); Paris, France (2005); and Potsdam, Germany (2007).

The July 23-29, 2008 negotiations in Geneva broke down after failing to reach a compromise on agricultural import rules. Brazil, Mexico and an alliance of developing nations—known as the "Group of 22"—had walked out of the negotiations when the EU and Japan attempted to turn the focus of negotiations to international investment rules and antitrust policies without first taking on the issue of farm-subsidy programs. Nevertheless, intense negotiations—most notably between the USA, China, and India— were held at the end of 2008 in order to agree on a protocol for further negotiations. Leading economic powers (the G-8, plus China, India, Brazil, Mexico, and South Africa) pledged to reach an accord by 2010. Time will tell if this timetable is realistic.

3. The World Trade Organization (WTO)

The **WTO** was created on January 1, 1995 to be the primary international organization regulating all matters of international trade.[17] The WTO was also designed to administer international investment accords. The WTO currently has more than 150 members and accounts for more than *97 percent of world trade*. Around 30 other countries, including perhaps most importantly the Russian Federation, are engaged in negotiations to become full members of the WTO. Specifically, the WTO was created in order to meet the following policy objectives:

---

[16] Following Cancun, the WTO determined that U.S. cotton subsidies were illegal. In subsequent negotiations, the United States agreed to cut farm subsidies for such crops as cotton, corn, rice, wheat and soybeans by 20%. Elizabeth Becker, "U.S. Will Cut Farm Subsidies in Trade Deal," *The New York Times* (on line), July 31, 2004, at http://www.nytimes.com/2004/07/31/business/worldbusiness/31geneva.html.

[17] *See* WTO, "An Introduction to the WTO," http://www.wto.org.

- Assist in the free flow of trade by reducing both tariff and non-tariff barriers;
- Negotiate further openings in world markets;
- Implement, administer, and carry out the various WTO Agreements; and
- Settle trade disputes between members.

Specifically, the WTO will meet its objectives by:

1. Providing market access to the products of other WTO members by lowering import tariffs on both industrial and agricultural goods;
2. In keeping with the philosophy of the GATT, encouraging trade with all member nations on a non-discriminatory basis;
3. Opening up *service* markets to foreign competition;
4. Providing effective intellectual property protection;
5. Instituting policies for attracting FDI;
6. Ensuring "transparency" in trading regimens by requiring the "listing" of all tariffs imposed;
7. Ensuring uniform application of trade policies; and
8. Placing restrictions on state-owned-enterprises (SOE's), in order to remove favorable national treatment and discrimination against foreign entities and foreign competition.

The foundation of the WTO is a concept called *normal trade relations.* This means that, in effect, a member of the WTO must extend the same favorable terms of trade (formerly called the "Most Favored Nations" Rule) to *all members* of the WTO that they unilaterally extend to any *one* member. The scope of the MFN principle includes customs duties and charges of any kind imposed on or in connection with the importation, exportation, and international transfer of payments for imports and exports; the method of levying such duties and charges; all rules and other formalities in connection with importation and exportation; and matters which cover internal taxes and regulatory laws.[18] Note that MFN rules applied only to products.

The actual text providing for MFN/normal trade relation status reads:

"Any advantage, favor, privilege or immunity granted by any member to any product originating in or destined for any other country shall be accorded immediately and unconditionally to the like product originating in or destined for the territories of all other members."

The web site of the WTO may be found at www.wto.org.

There are two major exceptions under the WTO:

---

[18] *See* Edwin I. Barber, "Investment-Trade Nexus," in *U.S. International Economic Policy* (Gary Clyde Hufbauer, ed.) (The International Law Institute, 1982), p. 12.

1. Developing countries' manufactured products may be given preferential treatment over those from industrial (developed) countries.[19]

2. Concessions granted to members within a regional trading alliance, such as the EU or NAFTA,[20] may be granted but may not been extended generally to countries outside of the trade alliance.

---

[19] The concept of a *Generalized System of Preferences* (GSP) was first introduced in the United Nations Conference on Trade and Development (UNCTAD) in 1964 for developing countries (LDCs). Through tariff preferences in developed countries, the LDCs claimed they would be able to increase their exports and foreign trade earnings that would be vital to economic transformation. Section 502 of the Trade Act of 1974 authorizes the President to designate a country or a territory as a *Beneficiary Developing Country* or BCD. The President was prohibited from designating any country for GSP benefits based on specific criteria. However, the President may waive certain conditions if he determines and reports to the Congress reasons that the designation of a particular country is in the "national economic interest." The exclusionary criteria included:

- In certain cases, the country is a communist country;
- Is a party to an arrangement that causes a serious disruption to the world economy;
- Affords "reverse preferences" to other developed countries which have or are likely to have a significant adverse effect on U.S. commerce;
- Has nationalized or expropriated U.S. property, unless "adequate and effective" compensation has been paid, negotiations are underway to provide such compensation, or a dispute over compensation is in arbitration;
- Fails to recognize as binding or to enforce arbitral awards in favor of the U.S.;
- Aids or abets by granting sanctuary from prosecution to any individual or group which has committed international terrorism; or
- Has not taken or is not taking steps to afford internationally recognized workers' rights to its domestic workers, as defined by 19 U.S.C. § 2467(4).

See generally House Committee on Ways and Means, 105th Cong., 1st Sess., *Overview and Compilation of U.S. Trade Statutes* (Comm. Print, June 25, 1997), pp. 12-19.

[20] NAFTA, which includes Canada, Mexico, and the United States, came into effect in 1994. NAFTA is an example of a free trade agreement (FTA) whose main goal is to abolish all tariffs between member countries. NAFTA also may be distinguished from a customs union which is a grouping of countries which agree to levy a common external tariff on goods imported from nonmembers. NAFTA covers the following subject areas:

- *Market access*, involving tariff and nontariff barriers, rules of origin, and government procurement;
- *Trade rules*, involving safeguards, subsidies, countervailing and antidumping duties, health and safety standards;
- *Services*, providing for the same safeguards for trade in services that exist for traditional trade in goods;
- *Investment*, establishing investment rules governing minority interests (the "golden share"), portfolio or traditional investments, real property, and majority-owned or controlled investments from NAFTA countries; in addition, NAFTA coverage would be extended to investments made by any company incorporated in NAFTA country, regardless of country of origin;
- *Intellectual property*, relating to creation, protection, and enforcement of intellectual property rights;
- *Dispute settlement*, providing for a process that will be followed by signatory countries, designed to keep countries from undertaking unilateral actions against an offending party.

See Linda M. Aguilar, "NAFTA: A Review of the Issues," *Economic Perspectives* (Federal Reserve Bank of Chicago, 1992), p. 14.

4. Dispute Settlement and the WTO: An Overview

Dispute settlement is a major component of the WTO—one that was lacking under the GATT, which contained no effective enforcement procedures. How does dispute settlement fit into the general organization of the WTO?[21]

The highest level of decision-making in the WTO is the *Ministerial Conference* which meets at least once every two years. The next level is the *General Council*, composed of ambassadors and the director of a country delegation, which meets on a regular basis. The General Council also meets as the *Trade Policy Review Body* and the *Dispute Settlement Body*. The next level includes the *Council for Trade in Goods*, the *Council for Trade in Services*, and the *Council for Trade-Related Intellectual Property Rights* (TRIPS). The WTO also includes several important "working groups" that deal with individual agreements and other areas such as the environment, development, membership applications, and regional trade agreements.

Under the WTO, trade agreements are considered essentially as *enforceable contracts*. The following represents the manner in which a dispute may be settled in procedures before the WTO:

First stage: consultation or negotiations (up to **60 days**). If an informal process fails, the parties can request the WTO director-general to mediate or try to help in any other manner.

Second stage: Upon a failure of consultations or negotiations, an "expert" panel of 3-5 individuals is constituted (up to **45 days** for a panel to be appointed, plus 6 months for the panel to conclude). The country whose policy is being challenged can block the creation of a panel once, but when the Dispute Settlement Body meets for a second time, the appointment of a panel can no longer be blocked—unless there is a consensus against appointing the panel.

Officially, the panel is serves as a resource for the Dispute Settlement Body. However, the report of the panel can only be rejected by consensus in the Dispute Settlement Body. As a practical matter, its conclusions are difficult to overturn. The panel's findings must be based on the agreements cited.

The panel's final report should normally be given to the parties to the dispute within six months. The WTO notes, however, that in cases of urgency, including those concerning perishable goods, the deadline may be shortened to three months.

---

21 Adapted from WTO, *Dispute Settlement*, http://www.wto.org/english/tratop_e/dispu_e/dispu_e.htm.

Panel Procedures

Each side in the dispute presents its case in writing to the panel before the first hearing. At the first hearing, the case for the complaining country and defense are heard. In addition, parties who have announced they have an "interest in the dispute" may be permitted to make their case. After the first hearing, the countries involved submit written rebuttals and present oral arguments. If one side to the dispute raises scientific or other technical matters, the panel may consult experts or appoint an expert review group to prepare an advisory report.

First draft: The panel submits the descriptive (factual and argument) sections of its report to the two sides to the dispute. Each side is accorded two weeks to comment. The first draft does not include findings and conclusions. Next, the panel submits an *interim report* to the two sides, including its findings and conclusions, giving the parties one week to ask for a review. The period of review must not exceed two weeks. During that time, the panel may hold additional meetings with the two sides in order to resolve the dispute. A *final report* is submitted to the two sides and three weeks later, it is circulated to all WTO members. If the panel concludes that the disputed trade measure or practice is in violation of a WTO agreement or obligation, it recommends that the measure or practice be made to conform to WTO rules. The panel may suggest a methodology for compliance which may include the imposition of *fines* or perhaps *trade sanctions*.

The report becomes the Dispute Settlement Body's ruling or recommendation within 60 days unless a consensus rejects it. Both sides can appeal the report.

The Appeal

Appeals have to be based on points of law. As in the American legal system, an appeal cannot seek to reexamine existing evidence or raise issues not raised in earlier procedures. An appeal is heard by three members of a permanent seven-member Appellate Body set up by the Dispute Settlement Body. This Appellate Body represents the broad range of WTO membership. Members of the Appellate Body serve a four-year term. Members of the Appellate Body are individuals with "recognized standing in the field of law and international trade," and should not be affiliated with any government.

The appeal can *uphold, modify, or reverse* the panel's legal findings and conclusions. Normally, the appellate process should not exceed 60 days, with an absolute maximum of 90 days. The Dispute Settlement Body is required to accept or reject the appeals report within 30 days. A rejection is only possible by consensus.

Two issues have been especially vexing: dumping and subsidization.

5. Issues of Dumping and Subsidies: An Introduction

Professor Raj Bhala suggests that "tariffs no longer matter in international trade law." He notes that in the period 1947 (when GATT entered into force) and 1994 (the eve of the entry into force of the Uruguay Round), average tariffs in industrial countries plunged from 40 percent to 6.3 percent. As a result of the Uruguay Round, the average tariff will fall to 3.9 percent and the percentage of industrial products receiving duty-free treatment will rise from 20 to 43 percent. Professor Bhala pivots from a traditional analysis and continues, "Non tariff barriers are what matters in late 20th and early 21st century international trade law."[22] As a consequence, two of the major complaints regularly raised in international trade negotiations are those of *dumping* and granting of unfair or illegal *subsidies* by a nation to a domestic industry.

Dumping

It is clear that export pricing is a very difficult process. The exporter must be careful to take into account unique export-related costs and include them in the final price quotation of goods. These costs are in addition to the normal costs shared with the domestic side. As noted by *Czinkota, Ronkainen, Moffett and Moynihan*, these special export (risk) considerations generally include:

- The cost of *modifying* the goods for foreign markets;
- *Operational costs* of the export operation. Examples cited are personnel, market research, additional shipping and insurance costs, communication costs with foreign customers, and overseas promotional costs.
- Costs incurred in *entering or penetrating* foreign markets. These costs include tariffs and import taxes; commercial credit risks and political risks associated with a buyer in a foreign market; and costs dealing in another than the exporter's domestic currency—foreign exchange risk.[23]

What happens when domestic production is challenged by less expensive imports? A question arises: Might some of these imports arrive in the domestic market as a result of foreign competition designed to *unfairly compete* with domestically produced goods? In more specific terms, have goods been literally dumped into the domestic market?

First, a legal definition is in order. Dumping is defined as the practice of exporting a product at a price lower than the price that the product normally or regularly commands in the domestic market or at a price lower than its actual cost to produce. There are significant accounting implications in any analysis of dumping because of special considerations associated with the practice of *transfer or intracompany pricing*—the practice of pricing sales to members of a corporate family.

---

22 Raj Bhala, "Rethinking Antidumping Law," *George Washington Journal of International Law and Economics*, Vol. 29 (1995), pp. 3-6, 8-23, in Raj Bhala, *International Trade Law: Theory and Practice* (2d ed., 2000), pp. 830-839.

23 *See generally*, Michael R. Czinkota, Ilkka A. Ronkainen, Michael H. Moffett & Eugene O. Moynihan, *Global Business* (2001), p. 440.

The difference between the price in the foreign market/cost of production and the price in the U.S. market is called the *dumping margin.*

In the United States, a domestic producer may petition the government to impose *antidumping duties* on any imports alleged to have been dumped in the American market. In order to qualify, proof must indicate:

- Predatory (intentional) and not merely unintentional dumping is actually occurring;
- The U.S. government can calculate "with reasonable specificity" the damage to its own companies; and
- The American government can show that the damage is significant (generally the petitioners must represent at least 25% of domestic production in any given industry.)

Because dumping is essentially an act by an individual company and not an act of a country, the WTO cannot punish a country in which the company accused of dumping is based. However, the situation may be quite different in a country that is organized under the model of central planning where the factors of production are owned or tightly controlled by the state. China, Viet Nam, Cambodia, Cuba and other economies similarly organized immediately come to mind.

If a company has engaged in dumping, it is incumbent upon the nation in which the company is located to take action against that company. If a nation fails to remedy the situation after proof of dumping has been made, the aggrieved country may legally impose an *antidumping duty on the product—in essence, it may place an additional tariff* on the imported product.

The number of antidumping cases indicates that dumping is indeed a real world problem but is an area that is fraught with definitional and proof problems.

Subsidies

The subsidies agreement negotiated under the Tokyo Round begins by defining a subsidy. Article 1 requires two elements: (1) a "financial contribution by a government or any public body" within that government territory, and (2) consequent conferral of "a benefit."[24] If a government believes that its products are suffering from unfair competition due to official government subsidies that a nation is "paying" or "allowing" to a domestic producer which *causes or threatens to cause serious prejudice to its interests*, a nation may

[24] *See* House of Representatives [Uruguay Round Trade Agreement], *Statement of Administrative Action, Agreement on Subsidies and Countervailing Measures*, H.R. Doc. No. 316, 103d Cong., 2d Sess., Vol. 1 (Sept. 27, 1994), pp. 911-923.

"retaliate" against such a product by charging a *countervailing duty to offset the subsidy*—in effect, an *additional tariff* placed on an imported product that has been receiving the unfair subsidy. These decisions are reviewable by the WTO.

Examples of subsidies may include the following: direct transfers of funds through grants or loans; assistance to a company through loan guarantees; foregoing of revenues through tax credits; or other price or income supports that target a specific enterprise or industry, specific groups of enterprises or industries, or enterprises in a particular sector or region. It appears that all nations engage in some form of subsidization or export promotion as a part of national economic policy. This area is fraught with political implications and a lack of precision in definition and scope of coverage.

Articles 3-9 of the Agreement establish a three-tiered framework for categorizing subsidies and subsidy remedies: (1) subsidies that are prohibited under all circumstances (the "Red Light" category); (2) subsidies that may be challenged in a WTO dispute settlement procedure and domestically countervailed if they cause adverse trade effects (the "Yellow Light" or "Dark Amber" subsidies); and (3) subsidies that are non-actionable and non-countervailable if they are structured according to criteria intended to limit their potential for causing trade distortions (the "Green Light" category").

In the United States, an industry, a manufacturer, or a trade union may file a petition with the *Import Administration and the United States International Trade Commission* (ITC) that will then conduct an investigation of the matter. Each country provides its own "list" of parties who may file a complaint. Antidumping duties and countervailing duties as trade remedies have been successfully pursued by a variety of domestic industries including producers of steel, industrial equipment, computer chips, agricultural products, textiles, chemicals, and consumer products. These twin issues will continue in importance in the future.

6. Trade Statistics for 2009

The following tables are taken from the official *"Foreign Trade Statistics"* garnered by the Foreign Trade Division of the United States Census Bureau. They will be helpful as a reference point for the essays which follow:

Total Trade (Goods)

Rank	Country	Exports (Year-to-Date)	Imports (Year-to-Date)	Total Trade (Year-to-Date)	Percent of Total Trade
---	**Total, All Countries**	**1,056.9**	**1,558.1**	**2,615.0**	**100.0%**
---	**Total, Top 15 Countries**	**735.9**	**1,141.7**	**1,877.6**	**71.8%**
1	Canada	204.7	224.9	429.6	16.4%
2	China	69.6	296.4	366.0	14.0%
3	Mexico	129.0	176.5	305.5	11.7%
4	Japan	51.2	95.9	147.1	5.6%
5	Federal Republic of Germany	43.3	71.3	114.6	4.4%
6	United Kingdom	45.7	47.5	93.2	3.6%
7	Korea, South	28.6	39.2	67.9	2.6%
8	France	26.5	34.0	60.6	2.3%
9	Netherlands	32.3	16.1	48.4	1.9%
10	Taiwan	18.4	28.4	46.8	1.8%
11	Brazil	26.2	20.1	46.2	1.8%
12	Italy	12.2	26.4	38.6	1.5%
13	Singapore	22.3	15.7	37.9	1.5%
14	India	16.5	21.2	37.6	1.4%
15	Venezuela	9.4	28.1	37.5	1.4%

Exports (Goods)

Rank	Country	Exports (Year-to-Date)	Percent of Total Exports
---	**Total, All Countries**	**1,056.9**	**100.0%**
---	**Total, Top 15 Countries**	**760.2**	**71.9%**
1	Canada	204.7	19.4%
2	Mexico	129.0	12.2%
3	China	69.6	6.6%
4	Japan	51.2	4.8%
5	United Kingdom	45.7	4.3%

6	Federal Republic of Germany	43.3	4.1%
7	Netherlands	32.3	3.1%
8	Korea, South	28.6	2.7%
9	France	26.5	2.5%
10	Brazil	26.2	2.5%
11	Singapore	22.3	2.1%
12	Belgium	21.6	2.0%
13	Hong Kong	21.1	2.0%
14	Australia	19.6	1.9%
15	Taiwan	18.4	1.7%

Imports (Goods)

Rank	Country	Imports (Year-to-Date)	Percent of Total Imports
---	**Total, All Countries**	**1,558.1**	**100.0%**
---	**Total, Top 15 Countries**	**1,163.3**	**74.7%**
1	China	296.4	19.0%
2	Canada	224.9	14.4%
3	Mexico	176.5	11.3%
4	Japan	95.9	6.2%
5	Federal Republic of Germany	71.3	4.6%
6	United Kingdom	47.5	3.0%
7	Korea, South	39.2	2.5%
8	France	34.0	2.2%
9	Taiwan	28.4	1.8%
10	Venezuela	28.1	1.8%
11	Ireland	28.1	1.8%
12	Italy	26.4	1.7%
13	Malaysia	23.3	1.5%
14	Saudi Arabia	22.0	1.4%
15	India	21.2	1.4%

CHAPTER 2

COMPULSORY LICENSING: A MAJOR ISSUE IN INTERNATIONAL TRADE TODAY?

Richard J. Hunter, Jr.
Héctor R. Lozada
Frank Giarratano and Daniel Jenkins

ABSTRACT

This article deals with the issue of compulsory licensing in the context of the TRIPS agreement, the Doha Declaration, and in connection with practices and activities in several developing nations. The article considers the genesis of compulsory licensing and its application to the pharmaceutical industry—a major component of international trade today.

INTRODUCTION

Compulsory licensing is a major intellectual property issue effecting international trade today, and will continue to do so for the foreseeable future. Escalating pressure emanating from the entertainment, pharmaceutical, and "high-tech" industries ultimately helped with the push towards a new international trade policy, culminating in the adoption of the TRIPS regime, discussed below. (Kim, 2007). Although compulsory licenses have played a large role in influencing all of these sectors, they have had perhaps the most important effect concerning how the intellectual property of pharmaceutical companies has been respected and enforced, most especially in *developing nations*.

Proponents of strong patent protection cite the enormous costs of bringing a drug to market, and argue "because of the scientific challenges of finding safe and effective drugs, only one of 5,000 new chemical compounds discovered in the laboratory ever makes it to market. In part because of the increasing complexity of the chronic and degenerative diseases that have become the main targets of pharmaceutical research, it now takes on average 10 to 15 years to bring a new drug from the laboratory to market, at a cost of more than $500 million." (PhRMA, 2009).

Astonishingly, approximately 17.6 million people in low- and middle-income (developing) countries will die each year from a variety of generally treatable communicable diseases and from a combination of maternal and neonatal conditions. It is interesting, but not all together surprising, that the occurrence of and the resulting death rates from these diseases and conditions are uniformly far lower in all high-income or developed countries. (Dutfield, 2008, p. 107, citing Dean T. Jamison et al., 2006, p. 59). These occurrences are primarily associated with a broad range of infectious diseases, issues relating to reproductive health, and childhood illnesses. Eight of these diseases and conditions account for 29 percent of all deaths in low- and middle-income countries. These diseases and conditions include TB, HIV/AIDS, diarrheal diseases, vaccine-preventable diseases of childhood, malaria, respiratory infections, maternal conditions, and neonatal deaths. (Dutfield, 2008, p. 107).

According to an article posted on *AIDS.org*, "Compulsory licensing—already widely used in the United States itself and in most other countries, and allowed under certain conditions by GATT and other international trade agreements—means that a nation's government, for an important public purpose, can allow the domestic use of a patent or other intellectual property, under terms and conditions which that government sets." (AIDS.org, 2007). The Paris Convention for the Protection of Industrial Property, which stands as the most important international treaty concerning patent right, stipulates: "Each country of the Union shall have the right to take legislative measures providing for the grant of compulsory licenses to prevent the abuses which might result from the exercise of the exclusive rights conferred by the patent, for example, failure to work." The United States is one of 173 countries that have ratified this treaty, effectively recognizing the right of a sovereign nation to grant a compulsory license.

James Love, an economist with the Consumer Project on Technology, notes that even in the United States, which has been a long-time critic of the process, compulsory licenses have been used in a wide variety of areas. For example, National Public Radio has a license as a non-commercial institution to play music on the radio; PBS does as well. In the biotech industry, the U.S. government has granted a number of compulsory licenses on key patents to other biotech and pharmaceutical companies. The U.S. Army uses compulsory licenses in such areas as satellite technology and night-vision glasses. (Singh, 1999). Under the *Clean Air Act* and its progeny, the U.S. government also uses compulsory licenses of certain air-pollution technology to promote clean air, and there are also compulsory licenses on aspects nuclear technology. These licenses are regularly granted on "public policy" or national security grounds. (AIDS.org, 2007).

Any opinion formulated concerning the issue of compulsory licensing, however, may depend on the *perspective* from which a party views the issue.

THE GENESIS OF COMPULSORY LICENSING

Professor Graham Dutfield notes that "In international law, compulsory licensing provisions arose in the late nineteenth century as a compromise between those countries that preferred to have patents revoked in cases of non-working, and other nations that were less keen to interfere with the freedom of patent holders to set up manufacturing facilities where they pleased." (Dutfield, 2008, p. 107). The general purposes behind the imposition of a compulsory license include:

- "To deal with a situation in which a patent owner is unwilling to work his invention (otherwise known as "patent suppression");
- To satisfy an unmet demand from the public for a patented product;
- To introduce price-reducing competition for important but expensive products, e.g., some drugs;

- To deal with a situation in which refusal to license a patent, or the imposition of unreasonable terms, is preventing the exploitation of another invention which is of technical or economic importance;
- To prevent abuses of patent rights including by breaking up competition-inhibiting monopolies and cartels; [and]
- To prevent the creation of potential competition-inhibiting monopolies and cartels." (Dutfield, 2008, p. 1).

As noted earlier, in 1994, the World Trade Organization approved an important treaty, *Trade-Related Aspects of Intellectual Property Rights* (TRIPS), which required all WTO member nations to adopt a set of regulations relating to the intellectual property rights as set forth in the treaty. In general, the TRIPS Agreement (Article 27.1) requires member countries to grant patent rights to the inventors of an invention in the field of technology on the condition that the inventions are *new, involve an "inventive step," and are capable of industrial application.* As part of TRIPS, all member nations were required to grant patents for pharmaceuticals for a minimum period of 20 years, which many developing countries had not been doing as a matter of practice.

Differing deadlines for complying with the treaty were established, with developing countries granted an extended period of time [transition period] to conform. Developing countries and economies in transition from central planning were not required to apply most provisions of the TRIPS Agreement until January 1, 2000. Least developed countries were originally given until January 1, 2006 to comply under Article 66.1. On November 30, 2005, WTO members agreed to extent the deadline until July 1, 2013, or to the date a country is no longer "least developed," if that occurs earlier.

However, for pharmaceuticals and agricultural chemicals, countries had two obligations. These nations had to allow inventors to *file* patent applications from January 1, 1995—even through the *decision* regarding whether or not to grant any patent need not be taken until the end of the period. This provision may be found in Article 70.8. This is sometimes referred to as the "mailbox provision." Secondly, if a government allowed such products to be marketed during this transition period, it had to provide the patent applicant an exclusive marketing right for the product for five years, or until a decision was made on the product patent, whichever was shorter. This provision may be found in Article 70.9. Thirteen WTO members notified the creation of "mailbox systems" to the TRIPS Council, indicating that they did not intend to grant patent protection to pharmaceutical products. This list included: Argentina, Brazil, Cuba, Egypt, India, Kuwait, Morocco, Pakistan, Paraguay, Tunisia, Turkey, United Arab Emirates, and Uruguay.

Several years later at the WTO Ministerial Conference in Doha, Qatar in 2001, member countries—largely responding to criticism launched by underdeveloped and certain developing nations—adopted an important declaration, *Doha Declaration of the TRIPS Agreement and Public Health*, in which they agreed that "TRIPS should not prevent members from taking measures to protect the public health of their citizens." (Canadian HIV/AIDS Legal Network, 2006, p. 2).

The *Doha Declaration* instituted several "loopholes" or what they considered as exceptions into the original TRIPS agreement, whereby countries could overcome unfair patent barriers. Two of these more popular loopholes are *parallel importing*, where a "country may import patented drugs from another country where the patent-holding manufacturer sells them for less," and *compulsory licensing*. (Canadian HIV/AIDS Legal Network, 2006, p. 2).

Compulsory licenses have been seen both as "cost-cutting" and "access-assuring" tools for developing countries to provide critical, often life-saving, medicines to their citizens. The TRIPS Agreement outlines the conditions under which a country is able to utilize a compulsory license. These conditions are found in Article 31.b of TRIPS.

First, a company seeking to produce a generic variety of a patented drug is required to seek a *voluntary license* from the company that currently holds the valid patent for the drug, in exchange for a royalty fee that is typically paid back to the patent-holder. (Canadian HIV/AIDS Legal Network, 2006, p. 2). If no agreement can be made with the patent-holder on "reasonable terms and conditions" and during a "reasonable period of time," then a compulsory license allows the company producing the generic drug to move forward with production of the drug *without* the consent of the patent-holder. (Canadian HIV/AIDS Legal Network, 2006, p. 2).

Many commentators believe that a major shortcoming of the TRIPS Agreement lies with fact that its language is vague concerning the meaning of the word "reasonable," and because it allows an *individual nation,* and not an objective, third party fact-finder, to determine what constitutes a "national emergency," a situation in which a nation would not be required to first negotiate with the patent-holder in order to procure a voluntary license on standard commercial terms.

While it may be presumed that the citizens of a developing nation would stand to benefit dramatically from the granting of a compulsory license to a generic drug manufacturer within the country, these licenses are unfortunately not always used for the attainment of a "public good" as intended. On December 6th, 2005 the Chairperson of the General Council made the following comment shortly after the approval of the *Doha Declaration*:

> "... Members recognize that the system that will be established by the amendment should be used in good faith to protect public health and without prejudice to paragraph 3 of the Article 31b (the requirement to contact the patent-holder about a voluntary license)...[and] not be an instrument to pursue industrial or commercial policy objectives." (WTO, 2005 (Chairperson's statement)).

However, as may be demonstrated, countries engaging in the compulsory license process have not always utilized these licenses to provide for *public health*, as the Chairperson had indicated should be the objective of granting a compulsory license. Several examples are expositive—but again may be viewed from different perspectives.

Thailand and India

Throughout 2006-2007, the Thailand military junta did a great deal of damage to the country's international reputation in terms of being able to attract foreign direct investment, as it stripped several Western businesses of their intellectual property protections. The military junta was responsible for "targeting highly innovative, economically valuable drugs produced by multinational companies, including cholesterol therapies among others, *without* correlation to public health pandemics or threats." (Finston, 2008). The Thailand scenario reflects how compulsory licenses can be abused as a short-term profit generation vehicle for a country, as opposed to providing a public health benefit as required under the terms of TRIPS.

There was, however, another less publicized side to the controversy. In an article posted on *AIDS.org,* the author refutes the assertion that there was not good cause for the Thai government's actions, and speaks out against governmental efforts in developed nations to protect patents and IP. The author states: "Despite this health emergency, the U.S. government has used its great economic powers to pressure Thailand to change its patent and trade laws in ways that will maintain this deprivation and make these and other patented medications even less accessible in the future." (AIDS.org, 2007).

The article further relates that the particular drug in question, *fluconazole*, could be sold in Thailand on a discounted basis for about 4% of its current cost, which would mean that everybody who needed this drug could afford to receive it. The article argues that many lives would be saved, at no cost to the patent holder, who would receive a small royalty (as opposed to receiving nothing when patients cannot buy the drug at all.) The author refers to the pharmaceutical industry as *proprietary*, and asserts that it strongly opposes any such relief, fearing precedents which could lead to weakening of intellectual property protections in more important markets—regardless of the specifics of each case, and regardless of the human costs of what Thailand considers "this abuse of U.S. state power." (AIDS.org, 2007).

The article continues:

> "... Thailand could use compulsory licensing to allow Thai companies to buy bulk fluconazole, ddI, or other essential medications from generic pharmaceutical manufacturers, sell the drug for use in Thailand, and pay a royalty to the patent holder (usually between 1% and 10% of sales); to protect the patent holder, the specific arrangements would be subject to review by the World Trade Organization (WTO) in Geneva, if challenged by a member country. But instead of letting such a case go to the WTO—which could set precedents, and almost certainly would bring more visibility to this way of bridging the treatment gap in poor countries--the U.S. pressured Thailand to change its patent laws in ways that will outlaw this possibility for that country. A balanced policy would still protect intellectual property, in order to preserve incentives

for corporate drug development. But it would ask that people in poor countries be required to contribute to profits only according to their ability to pay—instead of being written off and left to die without treatment (while contributing nothing at all to financing drug development, because they are asked to pay an impossible price which prohibits any sale)." (AIDS.org, 2007).

It is also interesting to note that the influential organization *Doctors Without Borders* (DWB) has voiced its "strong support" for the Thai government's decision to issue compulsory licenses for production of three drugs for the treatment of AIDS and a cardiovascular treatment on public health and public policy grounds. (People's Daily Online, 2007).

India has also benefited significantly from the use of compulsory licensing within the country. The generic drug industry in India has flourished due to a lack of patent protection for products patented in other countries, and to the recent compulsory license provision that was added to the *Indian Patent Act of 1970* that has been responsible for bringing in the generic drugs that India has not been unable to manufacture. (Sands, 2006). Similar to the case of Thailand, many analysts question whether India's use of compulsory licenses has been strictly altruistic or has it been used for the benefit of the "exporting country's commercial interests," which under Article 30 of TRIPS, surprisingly allows WTO members to continue to export to a country that grants a compulsory license, even for an illegitimate purpose. This has been considered a major flow in the TRIPS Agreement.

Reflecting on its status as a major developing nation (especially in the service sector), India itself has been a bit schizophrenic about the issue, allowing many pharmaceutical giants to breathe a temporary sigh of relief as the Indian government has approached the issue on a piecemeal, case-by-case basis, choosing to hold off on the wide-spread use of compulsory licenses unless it is faced with an "epidemic-like situation." (Choudhary & Singh, 2008).

A senior official voices the opinion that the sanctity of a patent gets diminished if compulsory licenses are overly utilized for reasons other than a widely accepted and documented national public health emergency. The Indian example seems to indicate that if a developing country is looking to attract significant foreign investment within its borders, it may not be in its best interest to issue a compulsory license, except under the most extreme of circumstances, as this practice will often indicate a broader lack of respect for intellectual property rights of developed nations. Such a practice could be detrimental to the long range plans and investment objectives of potential investors. (Kim, 2007).

The Brazilian Example and the Surprising Indian Connection

An interesting example of compulsory licensing occurred in May of 2007. The Brazilian government issued a compulsory license allowing the import of generic versions of the HIV drug, *efavirenz*, after the drug's patent holder, Merck & Co., failed to match the 60% price reduction requested by the Brazilian government. Merck issued the following statement: "As the world's 12th largest economy, Brazil has a greater capacity to pay for HIV medicines than countries that are poorer or harder hit by the disease." (Alcorn, 2007). It was reported that the Brazilian government has consistently sought lower prices for antiretroviral drugs in order to cap the cost of its national HIV treatment program, which provides free access to anti-HIV treatment for 180,000 Brazilians. It was estimated that 370,000 to 1 million Brazilians are currently HIV-positive. (Alcorn, 2007).

By reducing the price per day from US $1.56 to $0.45 by buying Indian generic products pre-qualified by the World Health Organization, the Brazilian government said it expected to save $30 million in 2007 and $237 million between 2007 and 2012 (when the official *efavirenz* patent expires).

President Luiz Inacio Lula da Silva, no general fan of western capitalism, stated: "From an ethical point of view the price difference is grotesque. And from a political point of view, it represents a lack of respect, as though a sick Brazilian is inferior." (Alcorn, 2007). The president was referring to the fact that in its negotiations, Merck was attempting to charge Brazil considerably more than it had charged Thailand in a similar deal.

Merck responded: "This expropriation of intellectual property sends a chilling signal to research-based companies about the attractiveness of undertaking risky research on diseases that affect the developing world, potentially hurting patients who may require new and innovative life-saving therapies." The spokesperson went on to say that Merck believes that "it is essential to price their medicines according to a *country's level of development and HIV burden,"* a solution that would have ensured equitable access to medications, and the ability of Merck to invest in future innovative medicines. (Alcorn, 2007, *italics added*).

In an editorial, the *Wall Street Journal* condemned the Brazilian move, stating further compulsory licenses would be "bad for intellectual property rights worldwide, and a disaster for the world's poor." (Alcorn, 2007, citing the *Wall Street Journal*). The compulsory license is a reason to be "downright worried," the editorial continued, commenting that drug patents are "only worth the paper they're printed on unless governments protect them," and adding that Brazil's move is a "slap in the face" to WTO regulations and to a market system for drug innovation. According to the *Journal*, developing new medications is a "risky business," and pharmaceutical companies will not be "willing to sink hundreds of millions of dollars into research and development, especially on diseases that affect the poor and sick in developing countries, if they fear their intellectual property will be stolen." (Alcorn, 2007).

In broader terms, and partly as a reaction to the examples cited above, many observers believe that compulsory licensing is simply not the answer to distributing medicines to the people of developing countries and that pharmaceutical companies are essentially being stripped of their intellectual property rights without adequate justification. Some in fact believe that proper access to medications in developing countries has nothing to do with intellectual property rights, compulsory licensing, or the TRIPS Agreement. Brian Ager of *Managing Intellectual Property*, claims:

> "The root cause of developing countries' inability to address their healthcare problems does not lie with the patenting system and their ability to grant compulsory licenses. More than 95% of drugs on the WHO Essential Drugs List (EDL) are not patent protected and yet one third of the world's population does not have regular access to these drugs.... The real reason for inadequate access to essential medicines therefore lies not with patents but with lack of international funding, a lack of political will and inadequate local healthcare infrastructure." (Ager, 2003).

Thus, it may be argued that it may be a practical, rather than an intellectual property, problem that the treatment for some of the most prevalent and known diseases such as malaria and tuberculosis are widely available at low cost, yet people are still denied access to them for a variety of alternative reasons, as Mr. Ager explained.

SOME TENTATIVE CONCLUSIONS

Governments of many developed nations and several pharmaceutical giants like Pfizer and Merck have continued to apply pressure on developing countries in order to limit compulsory licensing. However, despite these pressures, many developing and least developing countries have triggered TRIPS provisions which permit them to grant compulsory licenses to produce and distribute generic medications.

In a major development, the United States has been a major participant in what has been termed "TRIPS-plus" and has directly joined the debate.

In order to adequately protect a nation's patents and other intellectual property, the U.S. has recently

> "... negotiated numerous bilateral and regional free trade agreements (FTAs) that impose what are known as 'TRIPS-plus' intellectual property rules, weakening or eliminating the public health safeguards allowed under TRIPS. Patented medicines thus have even higher levels of intellectual property protection than required under TRIPS, delaying the availability of affordable generics. The USA has also pressured countries for greater patent protection through threats of trade sanctions and through the WTO accession process." (Oxfam International, 2007, p. 2).

The U.S. government has not been alone in this fight, however. Pfizer has gone on record challenging the government of the Philippines' right to use TRIPS safeguards in order to distribute a generic version of their hypertension drug, *Norvasc.* (Oxfam International, 2007, p. 3).

The examples discussed above, however, have fueled an important policy debate. It may be argued that issuing a compulsory license does nothing but ultimately harm the nation that engages in the practice and ultimately hinders product innovation on a far greater scale.

It may be evident that obtaining intellectual property rights through research and development activities, and paying to protect them, may not hold a high value to a business faced with situation of defending a compulsory license. It may be argued that the incentive to innovate and create new works that are based on effective intellectual property protection may be diminished as a result of both compulsory licensing and pharmaceutical arbitrage. Patent protection has a direct effect on pharmaceutical innovation. An example of this may be seen in the decade after the enactment of the *Orphan Drug Act of 1983*, which provided limited market exclusivity and tax credits for drugs for small patient populations, 99 drugs for rare diseases were marketed, up from 10 in the decade before enactment. In addition, internationally, pharmaceutical research and development increased by more than 600 percent in the decade after Italy's patent law was strengthened. And after Canada improved its patent laws in 1987, pharmaceutical R&D rose from 6 percent to 10.6 percent of sales in four years. In a 1988 World Bank study of 12 industries, it was estimated that 65 percent of drug products would not have been introduced without adequate patent protection. (PhRMA, 2009).

Compulsory license has clearly played a role in affecting how the intellectual property rights of international businesses are observed, protected, and implemented. However, the policy question remains: how can the developed world lessen the negative effects that these licenses exert on pharmaceutical businesses, while still promoting the distribution of drugs to those in need in a socially responsible manner? Katherine Sands, writing in the *Houston Journal of International Law,* notes:

> "There is an inherent conflict between protecting patent rights and protecting a right to health. In order to connect the two concepts, we need to find a concept that bridges the gap itself. Compulsory licensing is one way to alleviate the tension because it creates competition and 'directly challenges the exclusive rights granted to the patent owner.'" (Sands, 2006, p. 1).

If compulsory licensing in its current form continues, and the number of instances in fact increases, many industry analysts suggest that fewer new medicines may be developed. In effect what happens as this system is abused is that giant pharmaceutical companies, and by implication, U.S. consumers, may be required to carry the burden of financing research and development activities for the rest of the world. It is difficult to determine what the *best, optimal, or most ethical solution* to this problem may be, although several have been presented over time. Perhaps the most interesting idea would be for the WTO itself to adopt proactively an objective, fact-based *socio-economic model,* which would be used to determine whether a nation would be eligible to grant a compulsory license. It may be argued that the adoption of such a proactive model would help prevent abuse of the TRIPS system and because just not any nation could use compulsory licenses to earn access to cheaper generic drugs. (Kim, 2007).

Ultimately, the stance taken on the issue of compulsory licensing, and the effect such licensing practices have on intellectual property in the international business environment—especially in relation to life-saving medications and other vital pharmaceutical products—must stem from whether the benefits of being able to provide vital medications to those in need overshadows the claims of monetary losses in terms of intellectual property infringement for pharmaceutical corporations who own or control the underlying patents.

CHAPTER 3

UNDERSTANDING AND NEGOTIATING THE PRODUCTS LIABILITY PITFALLS OF OUTSOURCING TO CHINA: SYSTEMIC FAILURES OR ISOLATED PRODUCT DEFECTS?

Aaron Gordon
Héctor R. Lozada
Richard Hunter, Jr.

ABSTRACT

This article deals with the important issues of product defects and product liability in the Chinese market. The paper takes a close look at the scope of the problem, looks at the systemic causes of product defects within the Chinese market, discusses various attempts to reform of the manufacturing and production systems, and provides practical managerial and legal precautions that can be taken in order to avoid some of the more serious pitfalls when dealing with China in the arena of international trade.

I. Introduction

2007 was a disastrous year for manufacturing and production in China. Despite a year of continued strong economic growth,[25] the harsh reality of Chinese product quality was thrust into stark perspective for U.S. consumers, entrepreneurs, importers, and managers alike. During 2007, there were five times as many recalls of products manufactured in China than in the previous year,[26] and more than 50% of all recalls issued by the United States Consumer Products Safety Commission were for products made in

---

[25] The Associated Press reported that China experienced a "sizzling" (but somehow "slowing") 11.5% growth in 2007. Associated Press, *Chinese economy slows to sizzling 11.5% growth*, Oct. 25, 2007, http://www.usatoday.com/money/world/2007-10-25-china-gdp_N.htm. Before the recent world-wide economic downturn, China had been on track to overtake Germany in December as the world's third-largest economy after the United States and Japan. However, *per capita* income for China's population of 1.3 billion people will continue to be far smaller than that of those developed economies. Zhoa Qizheng, a spokesman for the second session of the 11th National Committee of the Chinese Political Consultative Conference, reported that it was possible that China could achieve an 8% GDP growth through 2008 despite a worldwide economic downturn. Growth for 2009 is a bit more problematic. *See*, *Spokesman: China can achieve 8% GDP growth through efforts*, CHINA DAILY, March 2, 2009, http://www.chinadaily.com.cn/bizchina/2009-03/02/content_7527011.htm.

[26] Michelle Fujimoto, Laurel Harbour, Greta McMorris & Erin Sparkuhl, *Importing Products: Risks and Defense Strategies*," 75 DEF. COUNS. J. 238-242 (July 2008).

China.[27] Many of the defective products have contributed to horrifying accidents or lasting health problems for the users or American consumers who have grown increasingly alarmed with widespread reports of injury, deaths, and damages. In spite of these consequences, affected consumers have had limited recourse and financial recompense due to the nature of the *closed* Chinese business and legal environment. However, what may be most surprising to legal and business analysts alike is that despite the alarming trend of recalls and poor product quality, there are no strong indications of a highly protectionist or negative reactions from U.S. consumers, corporations, and the government. The Wal-Mart experience is especially instructive.[28]

Wal-Mart noted in its 2004 annual report, at least 70% of non-food items sold at Wal-Mart had a Chinese component. Further, Wal-Mart imported an estimated $18 billion in products from China during that same year.[29] As the American Federation of Labor noted in its blog in June of 2007, "the U.S. trade deficit with China reached a whopping $233 billion [in 2006], ... imports for Wal-Mart alone accounted for $27 billion—11 percent of that total."[30] Interestingly, following the 2007 incidents, while overall world-wide imports into the United States may have been reduced, the U.S. retailer announced no change to its Chinese import stream and planned to continue to purchase and import a wide variety of Chinese-made products.[31]

The reason for such a slavish dependence on China seems abundantly clear: Many Americans are simply unwilling to give up the low costs and prices that China affords our consumption-driven society, especially during weak economic times. For many entrepreneurs and business managers, relying on the low-cost Chinese supply chain is

---

27 Michelle Fujimoto, Laurel Harbour, Greta McMorris & Erin Sparkuhl, *Importing Products: Risks and Defense Strategies*," 75 DEF. COUNS. J. 238-242 (July 2008).

Included on the list of recalled children's products were 142,000 Halloween pails, containing amounts of lead that violate U.S. standards for lead paint, 20 million toys, 80,000 plastic miniature football bobble heads, toy garden tools, 110,000 children's flashing rings, other children's jewelry and cake decorations, again containing lead.

28 Wal-Mart came to China in 1996. The first Supercenter and SAM'S CLUB were opened in Shenzhen, Guangdong Province. There are currently 104 units in 55 cities, including 99 Supercenters, 3 SAM'S CLUBs, and 2 Neighborhood Markets. Across China Wal-Mart employs over 50,000 Chinese associates.

29 Walmart Watch, *Wal-Mart China: Cozy Multi-Billion Dollar Bedfellows*, July 11, 2005, http://walmartwatch.com/press/resleases/wal_mart_china_cocy_multi_billion-dollar-bedfellows.http.

30 James Park, *Wal-Mart's China Imports Cost Nearly 200,000 U.S. Jobs*, June 27, 2007, http://blog.aflcio.org/2007/06/27/wal-marts-china-imports-cost-200000-us-jobs/html. At present, Wal-Mart sales account for 15% of U.S. imports of consumer goods from China. *See* Emek Basker & Pham Hoang Van, *Wal-Mart as Catalyst to U.S.-China Trade*, http://ideas.repec.org/p/umc/wpaper/o710.html.

31 *See* Doug A. McIntyre, *China Export Drop Signals Deepening U.S. Recession*, Feb. 11,2009, http://247wallst.com/2009/02/11. The author notes: "China's exports declined 17.5% to $90.45 billion in January. By some measures, this is the biggest drop in a decade. For the same period, China's imports plunged 43.1% to $51.34 billion." *Id.*

simply unavoidable. Given this "*addictive reality*," American managers must apply individual product or sectoral "due diligence" and must be sufficiently prepared to continue to purchase consumer goods and outsource manufacturing operations from China—but on much different terms. Managers will need to understand the scope and nature of recent product quality problems, be aware of the actions being taken by the U.S. and Chinese governments to modernize the regulatory environment, and recognize the managerial and legal precautions that can protect businesses from the products liability pitfalls of outsourcing manufacturing to China.

II. Understanding the Scope of the Problem

"Poor quality" fails to fully and accurately describe the recent spate of recalls stemming from Chinese manufactured products. The words simply do not capture the gravity of the defects or their potential (or in some cases, realized) consequences. Examples abound. American toy-giant Mattel had to pull 1.5 million toys from the shelves because of exceedingly high lead content in paint. Pet food imported from China was found to contain melamine, a chemical used to make plastics, fertilizer, and fire retardant. The chemical ultimately contributed to the death of hundreds of pets in the United States. Toothpaste from China was found to contain diethylene glycol, a substance found primarily in antifreeze, which damages the central nervous system, the kidneys, and the liver if ingested in large enough quantities. Nearly a half-million tires imported from China were found to be missing the strip that binds the belts together; tread separation-related accidents were the consequence. Chinese seafood has been found to contain a harmful anti-microbial agent that is carcinogenic. These are only some of the more publicized recalls, but the point is clear. As dependency on Chinese manufacturers has grown, their product quality has been found to be dangerously (or deadly) substandard.[32]

An investigation into the scope of the Chinese "product problem" also highlights the fact that quality and safety issues are not limited to export goods alone. In fact, goods manufactured in China for *domestic consumption* have been determined by regulators to be considerably *more hazardous* than export goods used in the United States.[33] In a nationwide survey conducted in China cited by David Barboza, nearly a fifth of the food and consumer products that have been checked were found to be substandard or tainted, demonstrating that the domestic risk is even more pronounced than the risk faced by importing countries.[34] The *Wall Street Journal* reported that the Chinese government itself had reviewed 114 types of products made for domestic consumption by more than 6,300 Chinese companies and found that nearly a fifth of these companies failed quality and

---

32 Thomas A. Sloma-Williams, *Helping China's Quality*, 46 QUALITY 104 (Sept. 2007).

33 *See* David Barboza, *China Finds Poor Quality In Its Stores*, INT'L HERALD TRIB., July 5, 2007, www.iht.com/articles/2007/07/05/business/05safety.php.

34 *Id.*

safety standards—the worst problems occurring in canned and preserved fruit and dried fish showing excessive levels of bacteria and potentially harmful additives.[35]

Some suggest that the domestic issues may have even been compounded by the heightened scrutiny of foreign countries.[36] For example, when diethylene glycol was discovered in certain types of toothpaste, exportation was halted but the products were still permitted to be sold domestically in order to fully sell out the stock.[37] Chinese officials seemed to downplay the crisis and stated: "This problem doesn't exist, it's just a matter of U.S. standards, [it's] not a safety problem."[38] However, in a survey conducted by the state-run *Xinhua News Agency*, 92% of Chinese respondents said they were "concerned about food safety," and 78% felt that government safety regulations are "not good."[39] These Chinese domestic issues should, however, not mitigate concern among American consumers or importing businesses. On the contrary, the domestic aspect of the issue should demonstrate the pervasiveness of Chinese product quality problems and the need for even greater vigilance and precaution when importing products into the United States.

Importers also must understand that the scope of the legal aspects of the problem is both expansive and complex. At the heart of the problem may exist a systemic flaw in the Chinese legal system. Fairclough notes rather incisively:

> China is still at the early stages of developing the type of product-liability and product–recall system that is common in many Western countries, a situation that leaves little recourse against companies that flout regulations that are rarely enforced. Product-liability lawsuits, common in the U.S., are rare in China's legal system. And there are no government regulations for the recall of products other than cars—though rules for recalls of hazardous toys and unsafe food are expected to be in place as soon as the end of the year.[40]

---

35 Gordon Fairclough, *China-Product Scare Hits Home, Too; Exports of Toxic Toothpaste Halted, But Government Lets Domestic Sales Go On*, WALL ST. J., July 20, 2007, at B1, *available at* http://online.wsj.com/article/SB118487371421671957.html.

36 *Id.*

37 *Id.*

38 *Id.* In fact, the Chinese Embassy in Washington noted that Americans should "deal with flaws in their own system before criticizing China, citing problems with U.S. contamination problems in spinach, lettuce and peanut butter over the past year." *Id.* Quoting further from the statement, "Certain isolated cases shouldn't be blown out of proportion to mislead the public into thinking that all food from China is unsafe." *Id.*

39 *Id.*

40 *Id.* For a discussion of the core deficiencies Chinese legal system, see Mark Blodgett, Richard J. Hunter, Jr. & Robert M. Hayden, *Foreign Direct Investment, Trade, and China's Competition Laws*, 37 DENV. J. INT'L L. & POL'Y 201 (Spring 2009).

Product recalls in 2007 resulted in considerable legal fallout in the form of class action lawsuits, multi-district litigation, shareholder lawsuits, and actions by attorneys-general from various states.[41] Understandably, most of these actions have not focused on manufacturers but on importers. The American Society of Quality has said that the legal climate in China provides no recourse for a failure to uphold terms of a contract, document forgery, or protection for intellectual property.[42] Further, in the United States, the *Consumer Product Safety Act of 1972*[43] grouped manufacturers, retailers, wholesalers, distributors, and private labelers into a single group of producers and marketers that can all be potentially liable for faulty products, regardless of their point of origin.[44] Simply stated, importers must be aware that "it's no defense to say, 'We didn't know' when foreign-made product defects lead to injury."[45] For example, when a recall of more than 500,000 Chinese-made tires occurred on account of tread separation issues, the importing company, Foreign Tire Sales in Union N.J., and the exporting company, Hangzhou Zhongce Rubber, were named in a wrongful death case. While both companies denied liability, Foreign Tire Sales, just like importers in most states, may potentially be held 100% liable for selling a dangerous foreign-made product.[46]

Compounding the issue of potential liability are the actions taken by China when a recall occurs and litigation subsequently ensues. Chinese "regulators" often shut down plants or entire companies as soon as severe defects are found, making it impossible to find a party in China to potentially implicate or to sue. For example, when melamine was discovered in U.S. pet food, the Food and Drug Administration (FDA) visited China within a month after the discovery to help determine the source of the chemical. When inspectors arrived at the factory, they found little evidence that the manufacturing company had ever existed, uncovering little more than a shuttered factory, previously known as the Binzhou Futian Biology Technology Factory.[47]

---

41 Fujimoto et al, *supra* note 26.

42 American Society of Quality, *Importers Share Responsibility for Unsafe Products*, BUS. WIRE, Jan. 9, 2008, www.asq.org/media-room/press-releases/2008/20080110-importers-share-responsibility.html. The group cited the following preventative measures as core components of any effective consumer protection regime: *increased on-site monitoring; reinforce discipline in supplier quality basics; look beyond price to relationship-building; and raise competency level of overseas suppliers.*

43 15 U.S.C. §§ 2051-2089 (1972).

44 Jeremy Quittner, *The China Code*, BUS. WK. Aug, 17, 2007, at 1, *available at* www.businessweek.com/smallbiz/content/aug2007/sb2007089_716295.htm.

45 Lorraine Woellert, *Made in China. Sued Here*, BUS. WK., July 2007, at 9, *available at* www.indianalawblog.com/archives/2007/07/law_recovering.html.

46 *Id.*

47 David Barboza, *When fakery turns fatal*, N.Y. TIMES, June 5, 2007, at C1.

Many experts suggest that plaintiffs simply refrain from even attempting to file a law suit in China given the swift "remediation" practices by the government, ineffective legal and regulatory systems, and the fact that Chinese manufacturers are "small, far-flung producers that can't afford to pay big judgments."[48] Even domestic Chinese product liability suits face insurmountable obstacles because of government actions. Not only are Chinese courts effectively "arms" of the communist party, but party officials often take a direct role in dealing with domestic victims in product liability cases, pressuring both legal counsel and their individual plaintiffs to refrain from litigation.[49] Ultimately, recognition of the scope of Chinese product quality issues and gaining a clear understanding of the complexity and near futility of liability suits in China is a strong first step for businesses attempting safely to negotiate outsourcing manufacturing to China, given the facts of the current business, legal, and regulatory environment.[50]

III. Understanding the Causes of the Problem

An understanding of the scope and complexity of the problem is only the first step for prudent importers; the root causes of the problem must also be appreciated. Ultimately, the reasons for the current crisis are two-fold. First, China has systemic problems in regards to its business, regulatory, and legal environments and its manufacturing industry is fundamentally ill-equipped to comply with the notion of quality control. China's manufacturing industry is deeply rooted in a culture of counterfeiting, a disregard for quality that has been exacerbated through the process of globalization, and the lack of control exerted by the owners of brands and the remote, often foreign, manufacturers of their goods.[51] Further, cutting corners is not "just a legacy of China's initial rush toward the free market" but it has become literally "woven into the fabric" of China's industrial

---

48 Woellert, *supra* note 45.

49 *See* Sky Canaves & Juliet Ye, *Chinese parents file milk lawsuit; couple's claim comes as officials oppose litigation*, WALL ST. J., October 1, 2008, at A21, *available at* www.online.wsj.com/article/SB122279824170891107.html. The authors noted: "Because courts aren't independent of the government, officials often take a direct role in dealing with victims in high-profile incidents. In the aftermath of the Sichuan earthquake, the parents of children who died in collapsed schools were dissuaded from turning to courts while the government conducted investigations." *Id.*

50 As early as 1999, China had announced a Five Year People's Court Reform Plan which sought to "improve China's court system by improving the expertise of judges, enforcing anticorruption regulations, allowing some discovery, and improving the efficiency and enforcement of judgments." *See* Stephanie M. Greene, *Protecting Well-Known Marks in China: Challenges for Foreign Mark Holders*," 15 AM. BUS. L.J. 382 (2008). It may seem ironic, but "The WTO does not require a member state to have a good legal system, ..., or even a fair one. Instead, it merely insists that foreigners and nationals are treated alike, for better or for worse." *See generally* Lindsay Wilson, *Investors Beware: The WTO Will Not Cure All Ills in China,* 2003 COLUM. BUS. L. REV. 1009 (2003). Attorney Wilson has identified three major "flash points" concerning Chinese legal institutions: (1) the lack of a cohesive legal "system;" (2) pervasive vagueness in the language of statutes and administrative rules; and (3) difficulty of enforcing judgments once they are obtained. *Id.*

51 Ken DeWoskin, *The 'Made in China' Stigma Shock*, 170 FAR EASTERN ECON. REV. 9 (2007).

economy.[52] Chinese officials are constantly under pressure to promote fast rates of economic growth[53] and continuously favor producers over interests of consumers.[54] It is generally accepted that voracious and cut-throat entrepreneurs find it very easy to take advantage of a weak legal system with virtually no regulations, and are essentially encouraged by a "business culture where bribery and corruption are rampant."[55] A visit to a Chinese factory brings to light other compounding factors.

Most industrial centers lack capital, technology or shear competence, and Chinese workers place a premium on obedience over quality, reflecting the "command and control" orientation of the closed communist system.[56] Additionally, the supply chain in the Chinese industrial environment is vast and industries can be comprised of hundreds of thousands of small factories, farms, traders, brokers, haulers and agents, all of whom maintain control at one point, but add little value overall. Strikingly, on average, it takes China *seventeen* separate parties to produce a product; comparatively, in the United States, it takes *three*![57] With every additional layer in the supply chain, effective quality control becomes more difficult. Although procedures and costs for quality control are well-established, Chinese companies thus far have had little incentive to institute a dedicated quality focus. Additionally, considerable capital will be required to hire qualified teams to document, implement, and monitor quality procedures. Incidentally, while the business culture and costs of quality control may be impediments to higher production and manufacturing standards, [58] the reality is that China's legal environment may stand as an even bigger obstruction.

China is still in the very early stages of developing regulatory bodies and a product liability and recall system that is common throughout Western or developed nations.[59] However, it must be recognized that product safety regimes in the United States and in other developed countries evolved out of responsible reactions to similar product quality issues. For example, as recent as 1937, more than 100 U.S. citizens died after

---

52 Barboza, *supra* note 47.

53 Current information relating to economic growth, investment, foreign trade, population, and other economic and political factors may be found in the *World Fact Book* published by the Central Intelligence Agency, *at* https://www.cia.gov/library/publications/the-world-factbook/rankorder/2007rank.html.

54 Edward Wong, *Courts Compound Pain of China's Tainted Milk*, N.Y. TIMES, Oct. 17, 2008, at A1.

55 Barboza, *supra* note 47.

56 Jeremy Haft, *The China Syndrome*, WALL ST. J., July 16, 2007, at A12.

57 *Id.*

58 *See, e.g.*, Francis Bassolino, *Sourcing from China: You get what you pay for*," MULTICHANNEL MERCHANT, April 1, 2008, *available at* www.multichannelmerchant.com/opsandfulfillment/archive/index3.html.

59 Fairclough, *supra* note 35.

taking antibiotics that contained diethylene glycol (the chemical discovered in Chinese toothpaste). The case paved the way for the passage of the *Federal Food, Drug and Cosmetic Act* in 1938[60] that ultimately broadened FDA oversight and established stronger regulatory responsibility and power for the government agency.[61]

The situation in China is vastly different. China only issued rules for recalling faulty automobiles in 2004 and established superficial recall regulations for food and toys in 2007.[62] However, the creation of a more comprehensive legal and regulatory structure will be critical in paving the way for systemic improvements in product quality and safety. However, currently, litigation against Chinese defendants is often a futile endeavor because understanding the network of middlemen and finding the party that actually caused the defect is nearly impossible. At the state level, Chinese courts are often unwilling to hand down decisions that allow foreign or domestic victims to recover damages at all.[63]

In fact, the government's official position tends to be outright denial of product quality issues altogether[64] and companies that produce poor quality rarely face financial penalties or public reprimand. Instead, industrial managers implicated in major scandals are often simply executed by Chinese government officials. For example, the *Associated Press/Reuters* reported that "A Chinese court... sentenced two men to death for their role in the production and sale of melamine-tainted milk that killed at least six children and made nearly 300,000 ill."[65] Under this system in which the suppression of lawsuits for the sake of social stability is prevalent, change will be difficult and slow.[66] Even when the government has implemented quality rules and regulations on exporting manufacturers, there is wide-spread evidence of what is called "product fade," where Chinese companies ensure that the first few product lots meet the required standards, and then quality gradually *fades* or decreases as material inputs are replaced with cheaper equivalents.[67] Ultimately, the sparse legal landscape and insufficient regulations in China,

---

60 21 U.S.C. § 301 (1938). The Act contains important definitions, a listing of prohibited acts and penalties, sections relating to food, and various general administrative provisions. *See* http://www.uvm.edu/susc/nusc237/ffdcatc.html.

61 Fairclough, *supra* note 35.

62 Loretta Chao, *Infant Illnesses Force Major Chinese Baby-Formula Recall; Kidney-Stone Cases Raise Questions on Product Safety*, WALL ST. J., Sept. 13, 2009, at A8, *available at* www.online.wsj.com/article/SB122122542993527897.html.

63 Patti Waldmeir, *Made in China but sued in America*, July 31, 2007, http://:us.ft.com/ftgateway/superpage.ft?news_id=fto073120071418327181.

64 DeWoskin, *supra* note 51.

65 Associated Pres/Reuters, *2 face execution over China milk scandal*, Jan. 22, 2009, www.msnbc.msn.com/id/28787126.

66 Economist Intelligence Unit, *Stoking Protectionism*, Aug. 16, 2007, at 1, www.econopmist.com.

67 *Id.*

coupled with the China's corrupt and irresponsible business culture, puts the onus for consumer safety on Western importers and regulators. However, many argue that this responsibility has not been taken seriously to date and the West's inaction has in itself become at least a secondary cause of poor Chinese product quality.

There are numerous critics who have indicted Western companies and regulatory bodies for complacency in regards to the scrutiny they place on the sources of cheap goods. In 2007, the FDA was only inspecting about *1 percent* of the imports that fell under its jurisdiction and still today many observers believe the agency misses most of the contaminated products that enter the country.[68] Additionally, only when repeated problems occur with a specific exporter does the FDA issue an official alert, which in turn activates heightened attention at the boarder.[69] However, the tracking database tied to this border monitoring system also has flaws that inhibit sufficient analysis and regulation. For example, the system does not currently store the *quantity* of a contaminated product that has arrived at the border; therefore, regulators do not know if an exporter shipped a box or an entire freighter of contaminated products when analyzing import data post-hoc.[70] Critics also argue that the FDA has not adapted to the deluge of imports in the last ten years due to expanding globalization. While an "Import Strategic Plan" was drawn up in 2003 as a means to restructure the agency and focus more resources on finding potential risks in the imported food supply, budgetary constraints have all but halted implementation.[71]

Regulatory bodies are not the only domestic contributor to the problem. Importers themselves have failed to share responsibility for ensuring safe Chinese-made products. Randy Gooden, chair of the American Society for Quality, notes, "Companies are so used to dealing with suppliers in the U.S. or Europe that comply with their specifications that they aren't taking into account that the whole concept of quality systems is a radically new thing to many foreign suppliers like China."[72] The most disciplined companies have "men on the ground" in exporting countries ensuring quality and providing training; however, many employees engaged in purchasing in large companies with vast layers of reporting structure have "lackadaisical attitudes" due to their lack of visibility. Alternately, many small and medium-sized businesses simply do not have the resources to monitor all their suppliers' activities.[73] Obviously, China itself should face much of the blame for manufacturing products of dangerously low quality;

---

68 Andrew Martin & Griff Palmer, *China not sole source of dubious food*, N.Y. TIMES, July 12, 2007, at C1, *available at* www.nytimes.com/2007/07/12/business/12imports.html.

69 *Id.*

70 *Id.*

71 *Id.*

72 American Society of Quality, *supra* note 42.

73 *Id.*

however, Western importers (regardless of their size) and regulators must also recognize their culpability for the failure to assure the importation of safe products regardless of their place of manufacture.

IV. Is the Problem Being Addressed?

In addition to understanding the scope of product quality problems in China and the causal factors, potential outsourcers should also review and monitor the concrete steps that China is taking to deal with product quality concerns. Internally, China claims it is making considerable changes in short order. Most notably, the Chinese State Food & Drug Administration (SFDA) has recently established an official Recall Management Methods program that if *completed, adhered to, and enforced*, may pave the way for national systems that will promote voluntary recalls and monitor industrial product safety.[74] It is quite apparent that "The American public is already aware of the dangers posed by many imported Chinese products. This is driven home every day by news stories on TV/newspapers about recalls of Chinese imports containing hazardous/toxic substances."[75] The $1.2 billion plan will channel funds toward building or upgrading the nation's quality and safety infrastructure by 2012, including drug and medical device testing centers.[76] In fact, China announced what effectively can be termed as a "blacklist" of 429 export companies that had violated existing regulations—including two companies that had been implicated in the recent pet food contamination scandals.[77]

In addition, a range of laws have been passed that suggest some legal steps are being made to modernize the regulatory environment. The *Product Quality Law*, the *Standardization Law*, the *Law on Import and Export Commodity Inspection*, and the *Food Safety Law* have all been enacted in recent years with the purported intent to improve quality and safety.[78] Vice Premier Wu Yi also noted that the government recently launched a nationwide campaign to improve quality and safety training in a range of areas, including agricultural products, food processing, food sold in stores, catering, medicine, pork, imports and exports, and other consumer goods involving health and safety.

While the ultimate effect of these laws may be open to question, given the corrupt culture and negative characteristics of the Chinese industrial economy, several concrete steps have also being undertaken. In 2007, the Chinese government and the United States signed the *Global Food Safety Initiative*.[79] At the very least this step signifies that China

---

74 Fujimoto et al, *supra* note 26.

75 *See* Esther D'Amico, *China: Flagging Up Quality Controls*, 169 CHEMICAL WK. 25, Sept. 2007, *available at* www.glgroup.com/NewsWatchPrefs/Print.aspx?pid=16647.

76 *Id.*

77 *Id.*

78 Wu Yi, *China Stands for Quality*, WALL ST. J., Dec. 11, 2007, at A27 (comments prepared by Chinese Vice-Premier Wu Yi for the Third China-US Strategic Economic Dialogue).

79 The objectives of the *Global Food Safety Initiative* or GFSI are:

has globally acknowledged the need to improve quality and is willing to do so via direct cooperation with importers.[80] The agreement addresses many specifics, including manufacturing, registration, and certification requirements, establishment of quality benchmarks, and the introduction of China's involvement in international regulatory and public-health agencies. However, while the framework to improve quality may be coming together both domestically and internationally, potential importers need to understand how far China remains from possessing an effective regulatory environment. As such, and for the foreseeable future, importers must actively monitor the legal, systemic, and industrial changes being made in order to sufficiently prepare and protect themselves from product liability problems.

V. Practical Managerial and Legal Precautions Necessary to Outsource From China

Finally, there are a number of practical steps in terms of supply chain management, contract design and insurance procurement that importers must take to protect themselves from the product liability pitfalls of outsourcing manufacturing to China. Michael Hausfeld of the law firm Cohen Milstein Hausfeld & Toll very directly comments on the need for adept supply chain management when he says, "Anyone relying on a Chinese manufacturer at the moment needs to do more than just put in an order and ask it to be filled. They have to take affirmative steps to assure the quality of the inputs."[81] Careful supplier selection with appropriate due diligence is an elemental step to supply chain management. Importing parties must understand the quality control and safety testing procedures of the manufacturer, whether products consistently meet specifications, whether facilities are clean and modern, whether management and employees are well trained and efficient and whether manufacturers outsource to other companies. Complete due diligence should also include checking the manufacturer's litigation and claims history, requesting references from other importers and investigating the manufacturer's finance and insurance status.

Subsequent to a meticulous supplier selection process, the American Society for Quality (ASQ) outlines four ongoing preventative measures that supply chain managers need to consider. First, increased on-site monitoring should be used as an on-the-ground presence can help to ensure specifications are being followed at each stage of manufacture and it can effectively manage corrective action when problems arise. On-site monitoring should also include periodic sample checks at multiple points through the manufacturing process and inspection of the supplier's books and records on an ongoing

---

- Create a convergence between food safety standards through maintaining a benchmarking process for food safety management schemes.
- Improve cost efficiency throughout the food supply chain through the common acceptance of GFSI recognized standards by retailers around the world.
- Provide a unique international stakeholder platform for networking, knowledge exchange, and sharing of best food safety practices and information.

80 Described in Fujimoto et al, *supra* note 26.

81 Waldemeir, *supra* note 63.

basis. Second, importers need to reinforce discipline in supplier quality basics. There are numerous resources available on the fundamentals of customer-supplier relations and these guidelines can help educate novice importers (such as entrepreneurs and small businesses) in order to avoid basic liability problems. Third, importers must look beyond price and focus on relationship-building. Supply chain expert Grace Duffy suggests, "Instead of focusing only on the cost savings of outsourcing to countries like China, importers need to do the work required to implement quality processes and build more long-term relationships with suppliers that will lead to fewer product issues and more repeat business and loyalty."[82] Lastly, ASQ advocates that importers need to work to raise the competency level of their overseas suppliers. U.S. companies can offer supplier development training to clearly outline their expectations, provide an understanding of their company's culture and assist the manufacturer in setting up a quality management system.

Next, manufacturer selection and ongoing supply chain management must be supplemented by a comprehensive supplier contracts that protect importers, particularly if a defects arise. Bruce T. Clark, an attorney that has represented plaintiffs in a number of food-borne illness cases says sloppy contracts lead to considerable problems for importers.[83] Broadly speaking, a good supplier should specify covenants, representations and warranties related to product quality, design, specifications, prototypes, samples, inspections and testing, all of which will impose on the Chinese supplier obligations to manufacture and deliver goods without safety defects. At the same time, contract provisions related to defects, insurance and indemnification should be used to outline the legal recourse against the Chinese supplier for a breach in the contract.[84]

Erika Schenk, leader of the commercial practice group of law firm Bryan Cave advises importers to describe everything is detail, noting what products will be tested on the site, by whom and who is responsible if something does go wrong.[85] Importantly Schenk says, "You want a contract where you are indemnified against lawsuits and claims, and one that would protect you from consequential damages if your business reputation is hurt."[86] Ryan Smethurst, an attorney with McDermott, Will & Emergy, goes further saying, "Importers must specify that the supplier's liability, including any duty to indemnify, is not limited to the extent of its potentially applicable insurance."[87] Attorney George von Mehren adds that the contract must cover foreseeable problems, even minor ones such as issues that might arise during shipping.[88] He adds that language should

---

82 American Society of Quality, *supra* note 42.

83 Dave Lenckus, *China recall crisis underscores risk*, 41 BUS. INS., Aug. 2007, at 1.

84 Grace Park Fremlin, *Careful Contracts Reduce Risk*, 35 CHINA BUS. REV. 34 (Jan./Feb. 2008).

85 Quitner, *supra* note 44.

86 *Id.*

87 Ryan S. Smethurst, *The High Cost of Low Prices*, 55 RISK MGMT. 20 (Apr. 2008).

88 Quitner, *supra* note 44.

be included in the contract that holds the manufacturer responsible for covering all the costs of any product recall, stipulates that the importer receives pre-production samples before agreeing to a complete run and outlines penalties for late or defective products. Lastly, it is advised that the contract include details that provide importers the right to return non-conforming products, permission to conduct facility, product and records inspections at any time and a dispute resolution clause.[89] Strategically designed supplier contracts are a critical aspect to negotiating the product liability pitfalls of outsourcing from China; however, according to Joe Underwood, a senior consultant with Albert Risk Management, too few companies have effectively "codified in print" an effective agreement that protects them if poor quality manufacturing arises.[90]

Lastly, in addition to effective supply chain management and contract design, the final precautionary element that importers must employ is insurance procurement both for themselves and their overseas manufacturers. In general, Chinese manufacturing firms do not carry much insurance (liability or otherwise). Therefore, within the contract, the importer should mandate that the Chinese supplier deliver a certificate of insurance that proves the manufacturer has purchased an agreed amount of product liability insurance with U.S. or worldwide coverage. The policy should name the U.S. buyer as an additional insured party and include a waiver of subrogation where the insurer relinquishes the right to hold a third party accountable for a loss suffered by an insured.[91] Importers must be wary of the fact that some firms in China have been known to purchase insurance coverage to fulfill a contract, and then cancel the policy once production is underway.[92] As such, the insurance portion of the contract should require that the U.S. buyer receive advance notice of any cancellation or non-renewal, and it should also state that the supplier is responsible for any deficiencies or gaps in coverage. Specifically under the policy, the legal costs incurred by the insured parties (manufacturer and importer) in defending product liability lawsuits must be covered. Additionally, the supplier's coverage should pay damages and claimants' costs and expenses that result from bodily injury or property damage arising from a defective product.[93]

Supplemental insurance policies should also be required. First, the supplier should be mandated to hold recall insurance coverage. This standalone policy (in addition to the aforementioned product liability insurance) covers the recall cost of the Chinese supplier and of the U.S. buyer, including the costs of replacing and repairing

---

89 David Blanchard & Jorge Perez Izquierdo, *Taming the Dragon*, INDUSTRY WK. Nov. 2007, at 28.

90 Lenckus, *supra* note 83.

91 *See* Fremlin, *supra* note 84.

92 Jim Gervang, *The China Question*, BUS. FIN. Oct. 2007, at 39.

93 Adapted from Fremlin, *supra* note 84.

recalled items.[94] Another important supplemental area of supplier coverage is EOIL or Employer's Occupational Injury Liability. Importers should require this insurance policy to be held by the manufacturer as it provides specific benefits to employees that are not covered under the national work injury program and protects against suits being brought against the manufacturer by its employees.[95]

Given a culture of corruption, U.S. importers need to ensure that manufacturer insurance policies are not only valid, but would be effective in case of a recall. As such, importers should establish relationships with reputable local insurance brokers to confirm their supplier's continuously maintain valid policies.[96] Importers should also consider requiring foreign suppliers to maintain some U.S. assets that can be attached if a product liability claim is filed; this partially protects against foreign suppliers simply shutting down abruptly with no notice after product quality problems emerges.[97]

U.S. importers should also have comprehensive liability insurance coverage. In fact, given the dramatic increase in the outsourcing of manufacturing to China, a range of new risk management insurance products has become available.[98] Integrated product liability packages, one of the newer products, provide a broad-based, one-stop solution which typically includes a risk management analysis of the supplier as well as product safety, design audit and product liability insurance.[99] Political risk insurance is another product for importers to consider. This insurance policy is designed to cover lost revenues if an overseas supplier folds for political reasons or suffers trade restrictions that affect or even eliminate the supply; the policy also protects importers against the costs for securing a replacement supplier and retooling its supply chain.[100]

Regardless of how well an importer understands the scope of and reasons for the Chinese product quality problem, the supply chain management steps, contract design elements and various forms of liability insurance described above are necessary to fully prepare for outsourcing manufacturing to China.

---

94 *Id.*

95 Gervang, *supra* note 92.

96 *Id.*

97 Lenckus, *supra* note 83.

98 Stephen Charnley, *Great Wall No Longer*, 75 CANADIAN UNDERWRITER 60 (March 2008).

99 *Id.*

100 Smethurst, *supra* note 87.

VI. Conclusion

China's product quality problems are undeniable. However, the evolution of the global economy has made outsourcing manufacturing from China a certainty for many businesses, both large and small. This inevitable relationship with China is fraught with liability pitfalls. China's business environment is by nature fragmented and corrupt, its legal and regulatory structures are miniscule and ineffective and many foreign business and countries have not taken the steps necessary to establish a culture of safe and defect-free production. While the current situation is less than ideal, potential importers should not categorically exclude Chinese manufacturers from their supply chain. By understanding the scope, source and evolution of the problem, and through disciplined and effective supply chain management, contract design and insurance coverage, importers can safely negotiate the products liability pitfalls of outsourcing product manufacturing to China.

CHAPTER 4

ANTIDUMPING LAWS SHOULD BE CONSIGNED TO THE HISTORY BOOKS

Robert W. McGee
And
Yeomin Yoon

ABSTRACT AND SUMMARY

Antidumping laws have existed in some form since the early twentieth century. Ostensibly aimed at protecting domestic producers from unfair trade practices, they have frequently been used as weapons of protectionism even when dumping has not occurred. When this happens, some special interest group gains at the expense of the general public. Studies have found that antidumping laws result in a negative-sum game, since the losses exceed the gains, an outcome that violates utilitarian ethical principles. Antidumping laws also violate property and contract rights, since they prevent consenting adults from trading the property they have for the property they want. This paper begins with a review of the theory and practice of antidumping laws, then proceeds to apply ethical principles to determine whether individuals who launch antidumping investigations are acting ethically and concludes that President Barack Obama "needs to be bold on trade" by starting out with correcting the popular view that "dumping" is bad and those who dump should be penalized. Frederic Bastiat pointed out the fallacy of this view in 1845, yet the view is not only still with many American politicians but widely believed to be true among U.S. domestic manufacturers. President Obama should proclaim the following: In a free enterprise economic system, domestic producers have no inherent claim on the funds of consumers. The only ethical way of obtaining consumer funds is through voluntary trade. Using the force of government to obtain the funds (by prohibiting foreign suppliers from competing) puts domestic producers in the role of the aggressor, and in fact makes consumers the real victims. That is exactly what happens when a domestic producer appeals to the government to request an anti-dumping investigation against some foreign producer that is merely taking away business. Therefore, all anti-dumping laws and policies should be abrogated to promote freer trade.

INTRODUCTION

> "Through the years, some men have discovered how to satisfy their wants at the expense of others without being accused of theft: they ask their government to do the stealing for them." (Curtiss, 1953, p. 19)

"Antidumping duties are … a bad idea… If Beijing wants to subsidize European consumers' shoe habits, by sending footwear halfway around the globe, it should be able to do so. Shoemaking is neither an industry with high barriers to entry, nor one where predatory pricing delivers an unfair competitive advantage… They encourage retaliation, moving international trade further in the wrong direction. The protection afforded by antidumping measures also encourages producers to focus on pleading or arguing for its continuance rather than concentrating on how to become more competitive themselves, … by moving to the top end of the market or even by becoming more responsive to customers' needs." (Editorial on "Anti-anti-dumping," *Financial Times*, November 20, 2009).

Antidumping laws, which penalize or prohibit foreign producers from selling their products in domestic markets for less than the cost of production or for less than the price they charge in their home market (Dolan and Lindsey, 1994), have been around for several generations in one form or another. In the United States, one of the earliest antidumping laws was included in the Revenue Act of 1916 (Knoll, 1987).[101] It was passed in response to alleged German predatory dumping during World War I (Dale: 12; Viner: 242-246). But antidumping laws were not used much in the United States until the 1970s, and were not used in most countries at all until the creation of the World Trade Organization (WTO). The creation of the WTO has made them more popular and their use is becoming widespread. As tariffs and quotas are reduced or eliminated, domestic producers are losing two of their main protectionist tools. Antidumping laws are starting to replace them as the protectionist tool of choice.

Antidumping laws have several advantages (if you are a domestic producer seeking protection) over tariffs and quotas. For one thing, they can be used to target specific companies, industries or countries. It might be called a rifle shot approach rather than a shotgun approach, which might better describe a tariff or quota. Another advantage, from the perspective of a domestic producer, is that there is no need to go running to the legislature to lobby them to pass protectionist legislation. There is no need to pressure Congress to raise some tariff or reduce some quota, which is both expensive and time-consuming for lobbyists to do.

The probability of success is also greater if one uses an antidumping law rather than a tariff or quota. In the case of a tariff or quota, it may take the legislature months or even years to pass the required legislation and there is a probability that the legislation will never pass. But with an antidumping law, the legislation is already in place. All that some group of domestic producers needs to do is file a petition with the U.S. Commerce Department, asking it to launch an investigation.

The "conviction" rate, if you can call it that, is more than 90 percent in the United States, which does not mean that nearly every foreign producer that is accused is actually guilty, but only that the system works in such a way that targeted companies, industries or countries find it difficult, if not impossible, to defend themselves. The procedures used in the United States have been said to be abusive by a number of commentators (Knoll: 1987;

---

[101] Some authors (Dale, 1980) point out that the Sherman Act of 1890 and the Wilson Tariff Act of 1894 could have been applied to antidumping situations.

Palmeter: 1986; McGee: 1993), including the United States General Accounting Office (1979). Yet the law not only remains on the books, with all its flaws, but also is becoming used increasingly to thwart competition and to protect domestic producers at the expense of the general public.

The three East Asian countries, China, Japan and South Korea, have become major targets of antidumping actions by the United States.

China

China has the largest population in the world, has great growth potential and is a low-cost producer. It was recently admitted to the WTO. It also has the distinction of being the most targeted country in the world and one of the countries most targeted by the U.S. antidumping laws in recent years. The range of products targeted is quite varied. Some of the products targeted by the United States include:[102]

Apple juice concentrate
Automotive replacement glass windshields
Brake rotors
Various kinds of carbon steel
Preserved mushrooms
Steel pipe
Coumarin
Folding gift boxes
Folding metal tables and chairs
Freshwater crawfish tailmeat
Fresh garlic
Glycine
Heavy forged hand tools
Honey
Pencils
Petroleum Wax Candles
Pure Magnesium
Silicon metal
Structural steel beams
Tapered roll bearings

If it were true that China sold so many products below cost, one might think the country was on the verge of bankruptcy. But such is not the case. China has one of the highest growth rates of any country in the world, which leads one to wonder whether there might be something wrong with the concept of cost when applied to antidumping petitions.

[102] International Trade Administration, http://www.ita.doc.gov/ia/webapotrack.nsf.

Japan

One might think that Japan would not have to worry about being accused of dumping, since its labor costs are far higher than those in emerging economies such as China and even higher than those of the US. But such is not the case. Japan was the second most targeted country on a worldwide basis. A wide range of Japanese products and industries has also been targeted, both on a worldwide basis and by the United States. Some of the products targeted by the United States include:[103]

Antifriction bearings
Certain hot-rolled carbon steel products
Clad steel plate
Color negative photo paper and chemical compounds
Corrosion-resistant carbon steel flat products
Electrolytic Manganese dioxide
Large newspaper printing presses and components thereof
Mechanical transfer presses
Roller chain other than bicycle
Stainless steel angle
Tapered roller bearings

Korea

South Korea is one of the Asian Tigers. On a worldwide basis, Korea ranks third in terms of the number of times it has been an antidumping target. Some of the Korean products targeted by the United States in recent years include:[104]

Various steel products
Dynamic Random Access Memory Semiconductors
Nitrile Rubber
Oil country tubular goods
Polyester staple fiber

Although more antidumping investigations have been initiated in the United States than in most other nations, the rest of the world is catching up (Boltuck and Litan, 1991; Messerlin, 1990; Nivola, 1993; Horlick, 1993). The United States, European Union, Canada and Australia were the primary initiators of antidumping actions until the mid-1990s (Bown 2007, p. 6). In recent years, more countries have adopted antidumping laws of their own, and they have stepped up the pace of initiating antidumping investigations. The Uruguay Round, rather than abolishing antidumping laws, strengthened them (Uruguay, 1993).

More than 120 countries took part in the Uruguay Round negotiations, which adopted new antidumping rules. Since the Uruguay Round reduced tariffs and repealed

---

[103] International Trade Administration, http://web.ita.doc.gov/ia/webapotrack.nsf.
[104] International Trade Administration, http://web.ita.doc.gov/ia/webapotrack.nsf.

most quotas, the antidumping laws have risen in importance over time, since they are now the most powerful tool that protectionists can use to keep out foreign products. There is evidence to suggest that antidumping laws have a strong negative effect on competition (Malhotra, 2006), a conclusion that can be arrived at a priori, since antidumping laws either prevent trade outright or make it more expensive to engage in trade.

Jallab and Kobak (2006) found that 68.2 percent of the antidumping investigations launched in the EU between 1998 and 2001 had a questionable economic basis. In other words, there was little or no economic justification for launching the investigation. The percentage they found for U.S. antidumping investigations was 76 percent. Their findings present strong evidence that antidumping investigations are launched not so much to prevent unfair trade (whatever that is) but rather to prevent competition. Another study suggests that at least some antidumping investigations were launched in retaliation (Feinberg and Reynolds, 2006), which is reasonable to expect, since antidumping investigations can be considered an act of economic war.

Table 1 shows the number of antidumping investigations launched by the 42 countries that were included in the Chad Bown (2010) database.

Table 1: Number of Antidumping Investigations Launched by Country

Rank	Country	Years Included	Number of Antidumping Investigations	% Of Total
1	United States	1980-2009	1227	21.0
2	European Union	1987-2009	707	12.1
3	India	1992-2009	588	10.1
4	Australia	1989-2009	489	8.4
5	Canada	1985-2009	364	6.2
6	South Africa	1992-2009	289	5.0
7	Mexico	1987-2009	275	4.7
8	Argentina	1996-2009	245	4.2
9	Brazil	1988-2009	238	4.1
10	Turkey	1989-2009	233	4.0
11	China	1997-2009	180	3.1
12	South Korea	1986-2009	142	2.4
13	Taiwan	1984-2009	126	2.2
14	Peru	1992-2009	123	2.1
15	Indonesia	1996-2009	83	1.4
16	Colombia	1991-2009	75	1.3
17	Egypt	1997-2009	63	1.1
18	Pakistan	2002-2009	53	0.9
19	New Zealand	1995-2009	49	0.8

20	Malaysia	1995-2009	43	0.7
21	Thailand	1996-2009	39	0.7
22	Israel	1995-2008	32	0.5
23	Venezuela	1992-2009	27	0.5
24	Philippines	1994-2009	21	0.4
25	Chile	1995-2009	18	0.3
26	Japan	1982-2009	14	0.2
26	Ukraine	2007-2009	14	0.2
28	Poland	1997-2003	12	0.2
29	Trinidad & Tobago	1997-2009	11	0.2
30	Costa Rica	1996-2009	10	0.2
31	Latvia	2001-2002	7	0.1
31	Lithuania	1999-2000	7	0.1
33	Uruguay	1997-2009	6	0.1
34	Jamaica	2000-2009	5	0.1
35	Ecuador	1998-2009	3	0.1
35	Czech Republic	1998-1999	3	0.1
35	Nicaragua	1997-1998	3	0.1
38	Paraguay	1999-2009	2	0.03
38	Panama	1998	2	0.03
40	Bulgaria	2002	1	0.02
40	Guatemala	1996	1	0.02
40	Slovenia	1999	1	0.02
	Total		**5831**	**100%**

The United States is far ahead in first place, with 1,227 of the 5831 antidumping investigations, which accounts for 21 percent of the total. The European Union is a distant second with 707 cases, followed by India, Australia and Canada. Fourteen countries had more than 100 investigations. The top five countries account for more than nearly 60% of all antidumping investigations.

Pie chart 1 shows the distribution for the top 5 countries.

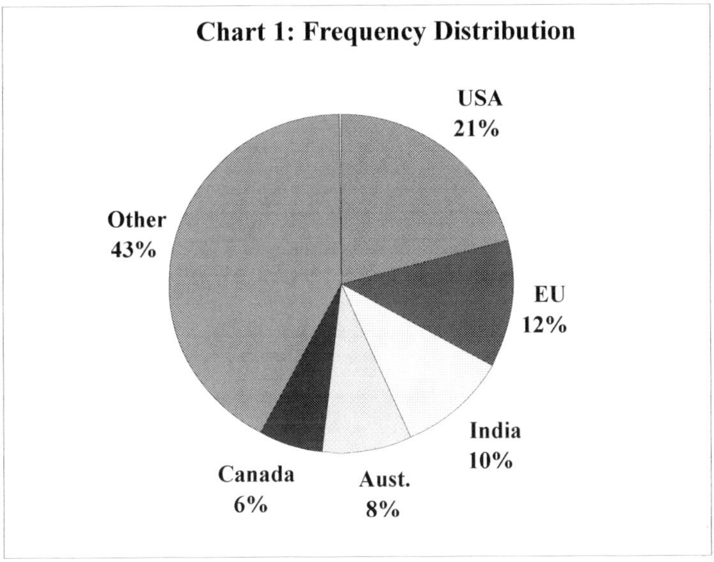

THEORETICAL AND PRACTICAL PROBLEMS WITH ALL ANTIDUMPING LAWS

One of the main theoretical problems with all antidumping laws is the premise that antidumping laws can remedy situations where there is unfair trade (Nivola, 1993). But where individuals -- willing buyers and willing sellers -- are able to trade what they have for what they want at a mutually agreed upon price, there can be no unfair trade. Unfair trade can occur only where willing buyers and willing sellers are not free to make deals without price, quantity or other restraints (Bovard, 1991; McGee, 1994). "Fair" trade has come to mean "the right to protection" (Finger, 1991; Salvatore, 1993).

One of the main arguments that has been put forth to justify antidumping laws is that they prevent predatory pricing (Boltuck and Litan, 1991; Kenen, 1994). Yet anyone familiar with the antitrust literature over the past few decades would find this to be a curious argument, indeed, since studies show that predatory pricing either does not exist, or if it does, it benefits consumers (Armentano, 1986, 1990; Koller, 1971; J. McGee, 1958; R. McGee, 1991; Nivola, 1993), which the antitrust laws are supposed to do anyway. Bovard (1991) points out that there are no known cases in the last hundred years where a company has dumped its products on the U. S. market, bankrupted domestic producers, then driven up prices and squeezed consumers for a long period of time. That being the case, it appears that the predatory pricing argument is not based on sound judgment. It certainly is not based on solid evidence.

Any antidumping law encourages foreign suppliers to increase their prices, since by doing so it may be possible to avoid triggering an antidumping action. The mere threat of an antidumping action chills price competition, since foreign suppliers will hesitate to compete too aggressively on price for fear of triggering an antidumping investigation. But no matter how hard they try to avoid such an action, they are not able to totally eliminate the possibility of an antidumping investigation even if they sell their product for the same price worldwide, because exchange rate fluctuations can make it appear that they are selling in foreign markets for prices that are below domestic market prices (McGee, 1993).

The existence of antidumping laws also makes it possible for domestic producers to charge higher prices than would otherwise be possible. That's because antidumping laws make it dangerous for foreign competitors to engage in aggressive price competition. As a result, domestic producers can raise their prices with little fear of being underpriced by foreign suppliers.

Any antidumping law is inherently protectionist because such laws benefit domestic producers at the expense of consumers by limiting foreign competition. There is no way to structure an antidumping law that is not protectionist. Discussions and debates about how antidumping laws should be changed, amended or reformed are therefore senseless. Yet the rules adopted in the Uruguay Round attempt to do just that. Commentators have concluded that any kind of major reform is unlikely, since the spread of antidumping laws has increased the number of constituencies that will resist any reforms (Moore, 2007).

There are also a number of practical problems with antidumping laws. The basic problem is trying to determine when dumping has occurred. The rules are not at all clear and there is much room to maneuver. Exchange rate shifts can subject companies to penalty even where the same price is charged worldwide. Computing the cost of production involves many problems under both the new and old rules. Which foreign market prices to compare with which domestic prices can also be a problem, especially when the products being compared are only similar but not identical.

Numerous antidumping actions have compared prices of dissimilar products. Sometimes these price comparisons take account of the differences and sometimes they don't. Price comparisons involving different markets are also not always good matches. Whether to classify certain costs as direct or indirect is not always clear, and the application of the allocation rules is not always consistent. Volume discounts and custom orders have not always been considered and the methodology the Commerce Department uses to compare foreign and domestic prices results in a consistent bias that tends to increase dumping margins (Bovard, 1991; Knoll, 1987; McGee, 1993, 1994).

THE ANTIDUMPING RULES

The antidumping provision incorporated in the Uruguay Round GATT agreement, could hamper trade for generations to come. Overzealous bureaucrats or domestic producers in need of protection have used and can still use these laws to the detriment of the general public. For example, profits, administrative and selling costs would be based on actual data pertaining to production and sales in the ordinary course of trade if such data is available. If not available, figures should be based on actual data from producers or exporters of similar products, the weighted average of other exporters' profits and costs for the same product, or any other reasonable method. This "any other reasonable method" gives bureaucrats a great deal of flexibility (and opportunity for abuse), since some methods used in the past that have been criticized have been considered by the government to be reasonable.

The effect that the new antidumping rules have on dumping margins and injury determinations is unclear. On the one hand, margins could be reduced if the calculation is based on a comparison of the weighted-average normal value home market price to the weighted average of all comparable export prices, or comparing transaction to transaction. But the new rules could also cause dumping margins to be higher than before. The U.S. rule required constructed value to include an 8 percent profit margin plus 10 percent overhead. While the new rules arguably eliminate this requirement, there is apparently nothing to prevent domestic producers in the U.S. from arguing that these calculations should continue to be used where it is the best information available. Using the EU's approach of ignoring third-country or home country sales when they are below cost and basing the profit percentage only on profitable sales could cause dumping margins to actually be higher than those that would result under the old U.S. 8 percent and 10 percent rules. There is a new rule for determining costs for start-up operations but it is unclear how this rule will affect practice and the determination of dumping margins.

The new antidumping rules add levels of bureaucracy and complexity, and adopt practices that have a tendency to inflate antidumping margins. It will also be more difficult to appeal an adverse ruling through the World Trade Organization dispute settlement process. There is nothing in the new rules to reduce the amount of abuse that has been going on for years. In fact, as the number of countries that adopt antidumping laws increases, it is likely that abuses will increase, as the antidumping weapon becomes available to domestic producers in more countries. The many ambiguities in the law will also increase the number of trade disputes, at least until the ambiguities are clarified.

ETHICAL ISSUES

Antidumping laws fail the ethical test whether one applies utilitarian ethical theory or rights theory. Utilitarian ethical theory holds that an act is ethical if it serves the greatest good for the greatest number or if the good outweighs the bad (Mill, 1962; Shaw, 1999). There is no doubt that antidumping laws are a negative-sum game. The losses exceed the gains. A few domestic producers benefit at the expense of the general public. Even the United States International Trade Commission (USITC), which oversees and enforces the antidumping laws in the United States, agrees that antidumping laws result in a net loss to society. Its 1995 study estimated that if all antidumping and countervailing duty orders had been removed, there would have been a net welfare gain of $1.59 billion, which represents 0.003% of the 1991 US gross domestic product.

The study grossly underestimated the cost of antidumping laws, for a number of reasons. For one, the study only measured the direct effects of antidumping laws. There are several secondary effects, none of which were investigated. In the case of antidumping cases involving the steel industry, for example, there are about 50 people who use steel for every person who produces steel, so merely measuring the effects of an antidumping investigation on the steel industry underestimates the amount of damage that the antidumping investigation inflicts. The 50 people who use steel must pay higher prices for steel products, but the cost effect on them was not measured.

Another reason the USITC study underestimated total damages to the US economy is that it measured only monetary costs. One goal of launching an antidumping investigation is to save jobs in the domestic industry. Sometimes targeting a foreign producer actually does result in saving jobs in the particular domestic industry that initiates the investigation. However, antidumping investigations can also result in job losses in the industries that use the product being investigated. Studies that measure the employment effects of tariffs and quotas have found that imposing trade restraints results in two or three or more jobs being lost for each job saved. If the same ratio applies to antidumping cases, and there is no reason to believe that the ratio would be any different, then antidumping investigations result in a net job loss. The USITC study measured only monetary losses, so nonmonetary losses such as job losses were not included.

The number of antidumping investigations has increased since the study was completed, both within the United States and worldwide, so the deadweight loss resulting from the launching of antidumping investigations is likely higher today than it was in 1995.

Although utilitarian approaches to ethics have some value, they are defective for a number of reasons. For one thing, it is impossible to accurately measure gains and losses. Who is to say whether the massive gains of a few domestic producers do not outweigh the minimal losses of each consumer in the aggregate? Of course, economists have devised methods to approximate the gains and losses, but the methods are only approximations. Furthermore, their econometric models are only as good as the data that goes into them. It is impossible to predict who the losers will be in some cases, since no one knows what consumers would do with the extra money they would have to spend in the absence of the higher prices caused by protectionism.

It is also impossible to compare interpersonal utilities. One may rank preferences but one may not compare one person's preferences against those of someone else (Rothbard, 2004, p. 258). But perhaps the fatal flaw in any utilitarian approach is the total disregard of rights. This defect can be overcome by applying rights theory.

Rights theory basically holds that an action is automatically wrong if it results in the violation of someone's rights. However, one may not say that an action is automatically ethical if no one's rights are violated. Certain acts may be unethical even if no one's rights are violated. One may only say that non-rights-violating acts between or among consenting adults should not be prohibited and that any law that prohibits such activity is wrong (McWilliams, 1996).

That being the case, we must now address the issue of whether it is ethical to ask the government to launch an antidumping investigation when the company making the request knows that dumping has not occurred. It is an important question to ask because companies often do ask government to launch an antidumping investigation, knowing that there has been no dumping. The mere launching of such an investigation causes competitors to either retreat from the market or raise their prices so they will not be found guilty of dumping. The obvious losers are consumers, who must now pay more for both foreign and domestic products. The less obvious losers are those who stand to lose their jobs as a result of decreased economic efficiency.

It seems clear that using government power to feather your own nest at the expense of the general public constitutes unethical conduct. If preventing consenting adults from entering into contracts would be unethical for an individual to do, it would also be unethical to hire some third party (like government) to do the job for you. If it is immoral for a principal to do something, it is also immoral for the agent to do it. One cannot escape a moral duty by delegating the task to an agent.

Even if "dumping" actually has occurred, the conclusion does not change. Consumers benefit if a company sells at a loss (which seldom happens because it is usually irrational to sell below cost). No one's rights are violated by allowing people to sell at a loss, but people's rights are violated if such sales are prohibited or punished. Thus, any prevention of trade constitutes unethical conduct, whether there has been dumping or not.

It is interesting to note that the ethical aspects of trade regulation are almost never mentioned by commentators. Perhaps the reason why the ethical aspect of trade, especially the rights aspect, is never mentioned is because most commentators do not see that there is a rights element. Yet the rights element is inescapable. As far back as 1690, John Locke pointed out that the body is property, and that the fruits of one's labor are mere extensions of the body (Locke, 1986). If individuals are not able to trade the fruits of their labor without restriction, their property rights are being violated. Yet that is exactly what happens when some government restricts peoples' ability to buy and sell, either through antidumping laws or with quotas, domestic content laws or other trade barriers. When the United States prohibits foreign products from crossing the border, the U.S. government is, in effect, violating the property rights of foreign workers. Repeated abuses of these rights could lead to retaliation and may lead to a chilling in international trade between nations.

Antidumping laws are weapons used by domestic producers to punish foreign competitors. The mere threat of an antidumping action places a chilling effect on trade and forces foreign producers to raise their prices lest they be punished for offering their products to domestic consumers for low prices.

Those who support the concept of antidumping laws either consciously take the position of special interests against that of the general public, or merely fail to distinguish the difference between competing interests and competing rights (Curtis, 1994). Domestic producers and foreign producers who want to sell in the domestic market have competing interests. If a foreign producer makes a sale in the domestic market, it is likely to be at the expense of a domestic producer, who loses a sale. It is a zero-sum game, since one's gain is the other's loss.

But there is no such thing as a zero-sum game when it comes to rights. Rights, properly understood, can never conflict. A foreign producer who makes a sale in the domestic market does not violate the rights of some domestic producer to make the sale because domestic producers are not entitled to sell to consumers who would rather buy from a foreign producer. Domestic producers have no claim, no property right, to the incomes of domestic consumers. Using the antidumping laws to limit consumer choices or to force them to pay higher prices as a condition of doing business is unethical. Forcing consumers to pay higher prices is like stealing their labor, since they must work more hours to earn the money to pay the higher prices that result from antidumping laws.

CONCLUDING COMMENTS

Antidumping laws increase costs, decrease efficiency and violate utilitarian ethics because the result is a negative sum game. A few special interests benefit at the expense of the great majority. They also must necessarily violate property and contract rights because they prohibit individuals from trading what they have for what they want. There is no way to reform the antidumping laws to eliminate these ethical deficiencies. The only way to end this special interest legislation is repeal.

A number of international economic experts such as Fred Bergsten, Director of the Peterson Institute of International Economics, have recently argued that President Barack Obama "needs to be bold on trade." (Bergsten, 2009) If President Obama really wants to be "bold on trade," he can start out by correcting the popular view that "dumping" is bad and those who "dump" should be penalized. Frederic Bastiat pointed out the fallacy of this view in 1845, yet the view is not only still with many American politicians but widely believed to be true among U.S. domestic manufacturers. President Obama should be audacious enough to proclaim the following: In a free enterprise economic system, domestic producers have no inherent claim on the funds of consumers. The only ethical way of obtaining consumer funds is through voluntary trade. Using the force of government to obtain the funds (by prohibiting foreign suppliers from competing) puts domestic producers in the role of the aggressor, and in fact makes the U.S. consumers the real victims. That is exactly what happens when a domestic producer appeals to the government to request an anti-dumping investigation against some foreign producer that is merely taking business away. Therefore, all anti-dumping laws and policies should be abrogated and consigned to the history books to promote freer trade. (McGee and Yoon, 2009)

CHAPTER 5

WTO: THE CONFLUENCE OF GLOBAL TRADE AND ENVIRONMENTAL PROTECTION

By

Richard J. Hunter, Jr.
And
Mark S. Blodgett

ABSTRACT

The confluence of global trade and environmental protection has perhaps reached an apex under the WTO.[105] *This article explores reasons for this dynamic combination in today's global economy and whether and/or to what extent it is warranted. After a review of the debate surrounding the relationship of trade agreements containing environmental provisions to the achievement of sustainable development, it then examines the costs and benefits of the WTO's environmental enforcement provisions. Can it be that environmental protection is a vital aspect of national wealth?*

1. Introduction

The confluence of international trade and the environment was brought under close public scrutiny and into sharp focus during the difficult NAFTA[106] negotiations, in which the United States aggressively insisted on negotiating "side" agreements with the government of Mexico in order to protect American citizens from environmental

---

105 The current membership of the WTO may be found at http://www.wto.org/english/thewto_e/whatis_e/tif_e/org6_e.htm (last accessed May 6, 2008). An organizational chart of the WTO is provided in Appendix I.

106 North American Free Trade Agreement, U.S.-Can.-Mex., Dec. 8, 1993, 32 I.L.M. 289 (1993) [hereinafter NAFTA]. NAFTA was approved by Congress by means of the North American Free Trade Agreement Implementation Act, Pub. L. No. 103-182, 107 Stat. 2057, 19 U.S.C. § 3311. NAFTA became effective on January 1, 1994. Exec. Order No. 12889, 58 Fed. Reg. 69,681 (Dec. 27, 1993). For an overview of the results of NAFTA, see Judith H. Bello & Alan F. Holmer, *The North American Free Trade Agreement: Its Major Provisions, Economic Benefits, and Overarching Implications*, *in* THE NORTH AMERICAN FREE TRADE AGREEMENT 5-7 (Judith H. Bello et al. eds., 1994). Another important issue was that of jobs. However, consider this statement. "Empirical estimates of NAFTA's impact on aggregate employment range from gains of 160,000 jobs to losses of 420,000 jobs." *See* RAJ BHALA, INTERNATIONAL TRADE LAW: THEORY AND PRACTICE 638 (2000) (citing U.S. International Trade Commission, *The Impact of the North American Free Trade Agreement on the U.S. Economy and Industries: A Three-Year Review* (U.S. ITC Pub. 3045, June 1997)).

degradation emanating from "Maquiladora"[107] production facilities.[108] Six years later, the debate had progressed well beyond the arguments raised during the NAFTA debate. "Environmental activists" staged a series of vocal protests at the 1999 WTO Ministerial meeting demanding the incorporation of environmental standards on the *WTO agenda*,[109] arguing that the inclusion of environmental standards in trade agreements would be the most effective way to assure that individual nations establish and enforce these standards.[110]

In retrospect, the 1999 negotiations had largely failed because of a combination either of a lack of will or a lack of real interest on the part of representatives from both the developed and industrialized world and less developed or newly industrialized countries. Industrialized nations asserted that the incorporation of a "tough" environmental regime would damage their prospects for continued growth, imposing costly technologies and processes which would further expose their competitive disadvantage vis-à-vis their manufacturing sectors. On the other side of the equation, many newly industrialized countries, sometimes referred to as NICs,[111] are in many cases

---

107 *See* Aureliano Gonzales Baz, *Manufacturing in Mexico: The Mexican In-Bond (Maquila) Program*, http://www.bancomext-mtl.com/invest/vox128/htm (last accessed May 2, 2008). The word "Maquiladora" is derived from colonial Mexico when "maquila" was the charge that millers collected for processing other people's grain. Today, the term is used to describe companies which process (assemble and/or transform in some way) components imported into Mexico, that in turn, are exported (usually to the United States). The website, "Made In Mexico," notes that "other synonymous terms are: Offshore operation, Production sharing, Twin plants, and In-Bond." *See* http://www.madeinmexicoinc.com/FAQs.htm (last accessed May 4, 2008).

108 *See* POLITICAL ECONOMY AND THE CHANGING GLOBAL ORDER 592 (Richard Stubbs & Geoffrey R.D. Underhill eds, 2006). For a discussion of the environmental side agreement, see Steve Charnovitz, *The NAFTA Environmental Side Agreement: Implications for Environmental Cooperation, Trade Policy, and American Treaty Making*, 8 TEMP. INT'L & COMP. L.J. 257, 260-283 (1994). *See also* Union Label & Service Trades Department, *Bill Would Axe NAFTA* (March/April 2008) (noting that Ohio Rep. Marcy Kaptur had introduced a bill in Congress that would require the President to withdraw the United States from NAFTA unless certain benchmarks—including targets relating to U.S. job growth, increased living standards, more U.S. domestic manufacturing, and stronger health and environmental standards—were met).

109 *See* STEVEN SURANOVIC, INTERNATIONAL LABOUR AND ENVIRONMENTAL STANDARDS AGREEMENTS: IS THIS FAIR TRADE? 231 (2002) (noting that "the 1999 Seattle WTO Ministerial meeting involved the inclusion of labour and environmental standards").

110 *Id.*

111 Newly industrialized nations include Hong Kong, Singapore, Taiwan, and South Korea—which are known as Asia's "Four Tigers"—Pakistan, Malaysia, Indonesia, Thailand, Mexico, Brazil, Chile, Venezuela, Israel, South Africa, and Hungary. *See The World's Economy*, http://www.infoplease.com/cig/economics/world-economies.html (last accessed May 8, 2008) (arguing that "Rather than take the three-world view, economists classify the world's economies as industrial or developed nations, newly industrialized nations, [and] developing nations.").

desperate for an infusion of foreign direct invention. Yet, they may regard the imposition of environmental standards by the developed world as just another form of economic protectionism, further eroding their chances from economic development.[112] Many newly industrialized countries also argued that the adoption and imposition of more stringent environmental standards would hinder their ability to be competitive in an international and globalized market,[113] although many of these nations recognize that the practices of foreign investors to keep costs and sometimes standards low are "a primary culprit in the social dislocation and negative environmental consequences that accompany globalization."[114]

At the same time, it is ironic that developing nations may be the strongest proponents of "free trade," asserting that "free trade" leads to welfare maximization and a general increase in wealth.[115] This view, however, is not universal. Professors Huang

---

[112] *See* PETER DICKEN, GLOBAL SHIFT: RESHAPING THE GLOBAL ECONOMIC MAP IN THE 21ST CENTURY 594 (2003). For a discussion of whether some standards may in fact be barriers to trade, see U.S. International Trade Commission, *Global Assessment of Standards Barriers to Trade in the Information Technology Industry*, Pub. No. 3141 (Staff Research Study 23, Nov. 1998). Article 2 of the GATT establishes the rules regarding the preparation, adoption, and application of technical regulations by member governments. Under Article 2.2 of the GATT, technical regulations are not to be more trade-restrictive than necessary to fulfill a legitimate objective, taking into account of the risks of non-fulfillment would create. Although the term "legitimate objective" is not defined, Article 2.2 provides an illustrative list of *legitimate objectives*:

- National security requirements;
- Prevention of consumer deception; and
- Protection of human health or safety, animal or plant life or health, or *the environment.*

See Uruguay Round Trade Agreement, *Statement of Administrative Action, Agreement on Technical Barriers to Trade*, H.R. Doc. No. 316, 103d Cong., 2d Sess., Vol. 1 776-789 (1994).

[113] SURANOVIC, *supra* note 109, at 239. World Bank member countries (185), and all other economies with populations of more than 30,000 (209 total) are grouped as follows: *low income*, $905 or less; *lower middle income*, $906 - $3,595; *upper middle income*, $3,596 - $11,115; and *high income*, $11,116 or more. Low-income and middle-income economies are sometimes referred to as developing economies. Economies are divided according to GNI (Gross National Income) per capita, calculated using the World Bank Atlas method. *See* The World Bank, *Country Classifications*, http://web.worldbank.org (last visited May 3, 2008).

[114] Stubbs & Underhill, eds, *supra* note 108, at 251.

[115] Free trade is a belief in which the trade flows of goods and services between or within countries should be unhindered by government-imposed restrictions such as taxes or tariffs, or other trade barriers such as quotas on imports, the imposition of illegitimate product standards, or improper subsidies for producers. Free trade is often said to encompass free access to markets, free access to market information, the inability of individual firms to distort markets through government-imposed monopoly or oligopoly power, the free movement of labor between and within countries, and the free movement of capital between and within countries. Adapted from *Encarta* (accessed May 8, 2008).

For a critique of the concept known as "fair trade," see ROBERT W. MCGEE, A TRADE POLICY FOR FREE SOCIETIES 13-14 (1994).

and Labys, for example, argue that free trade may not always be the panacea it is advertised to be, asserting that "free trade" at the expense of environmental degradation in fact *lowers* welfare maximization.[116] Although the traditional basis for international trade—comparative advantage[117]—might actually encourage a country to manufacture a "pollution intensive commodity," this type of production will inevitably contribute to the deterioration of a country's long-term environmental quality,[118] yet provide a much needed immediate or short-term capital infusion. As Huang and Labys noted:

> There is a trade off between gains from trade and environmental deterioration in this country, compared to a country producing non-polluting goods, since income will increase only if gains from trade over-compensate welfare losses from environmental damage. Stricter environmental policies in the first country would thus affect its comparative advantage and consequently its economic growth.[119]

Stubbs and Underhill concur that trade liberalization in fact undermines the environment and sabotages international environmental agreements, while significantly exacerbating ecological damages.[120] In order to implement transnational or worldwide standards, proponents of what we term a "*worldwide environmental ethical imperative*" propose that the WTO extend its mandate to include trade sanctions in environmental treaties.[121] Opponents of standards contend, on the other hand, that WTO rules do not

---

116 *See* Haixiao Huang & Walter C. Labys, *Environment and Trade: A Review of Issues and Methods*, 2 INT'L J. GLOBAL ENVTL. ISSUES 100 (2002), *available at* http://www.rri.wvu.edu/pdffilesd/labys2001-1.pdf (last accessed May 3, 2008).

117 Comparative advantage exists when a country has an advantage or a *margin of superiority* in the production of a good or service. The basic theory of comparative advantage was developed by the British economist, David Ricardo (1772-1823). Ricardo's theory of comparative advantage was further developed by economists Eli Heckscher, Bertil Ohlin, and Paul Samuelson who argued that countries have different factor endowments (factors of production) of labor, land, and capital inputs. Countries should bases their economic decisions on comparative advantage by first specializing and producing and then exporting only those products which use the factors of production which they are most endowed in the best possible ways. In terms of international trade, if each country specializes in producing and exporting those goods and services where they have a comparative advantage, then total output and the general economic welfare of all nations can be increased. *See tutor2u,* http://www.tutor2u.net) (last accessed May 4, 2008).

For a critique of the theory of comparative advantage and a discussion of "the new trade theory," see Paul Krugman, *Empirical Evidence of the New Trade Theories: The Current State of Play*, *in* NEW TRADE THEORIES: A LOOK AT THE EMPIRICAL EVIDENCE 12-23 (Center for Economic Policy Research, Bocconi University, Milan ed., 1994).

118 Huang & Labys, *supra* note 116, at 163.

119 *Id.*

120 *See* Stubbs & Underhill, *supra* note 108, at 111.

121 SURANOVIC, *supra* note 109, at 241.

hinder the ability of sovereign nations[122] from adopting environmental standards through the normal treaty process because environmental issues are already considered and have been sanctioned by the WTO Committee on Trade and Environment (CTE).[123] For example, opponents of *imposed* worldwide environmental standards point to the 1987 *Montreal Protocol on Substances that Deplete the Ozone Layer,*[124] the 1973 *Convention on International Trade in Endangered Species of Flora and Fauna,*[125] the *Convention on Biological Diversity,*[126] the *Framework Convention on Climate Change,*[127] and the *Kyoto Protocol on Climate Change*[128] as examples of voluntary international environmental agreements that are fully consistent with WTO principles.[129]

II. Background: Trade and Development

There is growing concern about the necessity for trade policies to address directly environmental issues. There is little doubt that the negative effects of environmental problems extend well beyond national borders. Professors Kubasek and Silverman[130]

---

122 The traditional characteristics of sovereignty generally are said to include:

- Independence of political and economic institutions;
- An effective governmental structure (including the existence of independent executive, legislative, and judicial branches);
- A defined physical territory;
- The capacity to enter into and conduct foreign relations; and
- A population.

See, e.g., Nkambo Mugerwa, *Subjects of International Law, in* MANUAL OF PUBLIC INTERNATIONAL LAW 253-255 (Max Sorensen ed., 1968). For a discussion of international trade and sovereignty, see GARY BURTLESS ET AL., GLOBAPHOBIA 110, 112-120 (1999).

123 SURANOVIC, *supra* note 109, at 241.

124 26 I.L.M. 1541 (1987).

125 Convention on International Trade in Endangered Species of Flora and Fauna (Mar. 3, 1973), 27 U.S.T. 1087. *See also* Convention on Biological Diversity, 1760 U.N.T.S. 79 (June 5, 1992), *available at* http://www.biodiv.org/convention/convention.shtml (providing another example of a voluntary agreement in the environmental area) (last accessed Sept. 10, 2008).

126 Convention on Biological Diversity, June 5, 1992, 1760 U.N.T.S. 79, 31 I.L.M. 818.

127 *See* United Nations Framework Convention on Climate Change art. 2, May 9, 1992, S. Treaty Doc. No. 102-38 (1992), 1771 U.N.T.S. 165, 168 (defining greenhouse gases as "natural and anthropogenic" gases in the atmosphere that "absorb and re-emit infrared radiation").

128 Kyoto Protocol to the United Nations Framework Convention on Climate Change, Dec. 10, 1997, 37 I.L.M. 22 (1998) [hereinafter Kyoto Protocol].

129 SURANOVIC, *supra* note 109, at 241.

130 NANCY K. KUBASEK & GARY S. SILVERMAN, ENVIRONMENTAL LAW 441 (2008).

note that recognition of this concept is "best exemplified by Principle 21 of the Stockholm Declaration" which reads:

> States have, in accordance with the Charter of the United Nations and the principles of international law, the *sovereign right* to exploit their own resources pursuant to their environmental principles, and the *responsibility* to ensure that activities within their jurisdiction or control do not cause damage to the environment of other states or areas beyond the limits of national jurisdiction.[131]

Three concrete examples are now well known. "Acid rain produced by certain types of energy-creation is carried by the wind beyond its points of origins to create environmental damage."[132] The ozone layer is damaged by "the use of certain chemicals that retain their stability over long periods of time and move upwards into the stratosphere, expelling chlorine that destroys ozone molecules."[133] And, greenhouse gasses have contributed to rising temperatures across the world. As a result of a recognition of these problems, environmental concerns have already lead to the creation of a *global regulatory regime* through the normal treaty process that addresses environmental issues that cannot be solved by the national legislatures of one country acting alone.

In particular, the Kyoto Protocol included environmental standards and provided sanctions against countries that do not adhere to these standards.[134] "Countries failing to meet their first set of targets by 2012 will have to add the shortfall to the next commitment period plus a 30 percent penalty. They will also be excluded from carbon trading and will have to take corrective measures at home."[135] Despite these facts, it is surprising that most developing countries assented to the Kyoto Accords[136]

---

131 *Id.* (italics added) (citing Article 21 of the Stockholm Declaration on the Human Environment). *See also* Louis Sohn, *The Stockholm Declaration on the Human Environment*, 14 HARV. J. ENVTL. L. 423 (1973).

132 DICKEN, *supra* note 112, at 595.

133 *Id.*

134 *Id.* at 596.

135 Carbon trading is itself very controversial. Emissions' trading is an attempt to provide an economic incentive for achieving reductions in the emissions of pollutants. The process is sometimes referred to as "**cap and trade**." A government or an international body sets a limit or *cap* on the total amount of a pollutant that can be emitted. Companies or other groups are issued *emission permits* and are required to hold an equivalent number of *allowances* (or *credits*) which represent the right to emit a specific amount of these pollutants. The total amount of allowances and credits cannot exceed the cap, limiting total emissions to that level. Companies that need to increase their emissions must effectively *buy credits* from those who pollute less. The transfer of allowances is referred to as a trade. In effect, the buyer is paying a charge for polluting, while the seller is being rewarded for having reduced emissions by more than was needed. Thus, in theory, those that can easily reduce emissions most cheaply will do so, achieving the pollution reduction at the lowest possible cost to society-at-large.

The most recent round of WTO negotiations, termed the Doha Round,[137] has refocused international attention on the convergence of trade and environmental issues and has also raised significant policy questions with regard to the relationship of trade and the environment *in the context of the WTO.* The Doha Round essentially provides members:

> ... a chance to achieve an even more efficient allocation of resources on a global scale through the continued reduction of obstacles to trade. The Round is also an opportunity to pursue win-win-win results for trade, development and the environment. For example, the Doha Round is the first time environmental issues have featured explicitly in the context of a multilateral trade negotiation and the overarching objective is to enhance the mutual supportiveness of trade and environment. Members are

---

[136] As of November 2007, 175 parties have ratified the protocol. Of these, 36 developed countries (plus the European Union as an entity) are required to reduce greenhouse gas emissions to the levels specified for each of them in the treaty—representing over 61.6% of emissions from a list termed *Annex I countries.* These countries have accepted greenhouse gas emission reduction obligations and must submit an annual greenhouse gas inventory. One hundred and thirty-seven (137) developing countries have ratified the protocol, including Brazil, China, and India, but have assumed no obligations beyond monitoring and reporting emissions at this time. This seeming dichotomy has proved a major flash-point of criticism for opponents of the Kyoto Protocol in the United States.

According to a press release from the United Nations Environment Programme:

> The Kyoto Protocol is an agreement under which industrialized countries will reduce their collective emissions of greenhouse gases by 5.2% compared to the year 1990 (but note that, compared to the emissions levels that would be expected by 2010 without the Protocol, this limitation represents a 29% cut). The goal is to lower overall emissions of six greenhouse gases - carbon dioxide, methane, nitrous oxide, sulfur hexafluoride, hydrofluorocarbons, and perfluorocarbons—averaged over the period of 2008-2012. National limitations range from 8% reductions for the European Union and some others to 7% for the US, 6% for Japan, 0% for Russia, and permitted increases of 8% for Australia and 10% for Iceland.

See United Nations Environment Programme, *Industrialized countries to cut greenhouse gas emissions by 5.2%* (Press release, Dec. 11, 1997) (last accessed May 5, 2008).

[137] The Doha Development Round commenced at Doha, Qatar in November 2001 and is still continuing. The objectives of this round of trade negotiations was to further lower trade barriers around the world, encouraging free trade between countries of varying economic backgrounds and stages of economic development. As of 2008, talks have stalled over a divide between the developed nations led by the European Union, the United States and Japan and several of the major developing countries (represented by the G20 developing nations), led and represented mainly by India, Brazil, China, and South Africa. Subsequent ministerial meetings took place in Cancún, Mexico (2003), and Hong Kong, China (2005). Related negotiations took place in Geneva, Switzerland; Paris, France; and again in Geneva. Adapted from *Doha Development Agenda: Negotiations, implementation and development*, http://www.wto.org (last accessed May 7, 2008).

> working to liberalize trade in goods and services that can benefit the environment. They are also discussing ways to maintain a harmonious co-existence between WTO rules and the specific trade obligations in various agreements that have been negotiated multilaterally to protect the environment. Other parts of the Doha negotiations are also relevant to the environment, for example aspects of the agriculture negotiations and also disciplines on fisheries subsidies. The Doha Development Agenda also has a section specifying the priority items in the CTE's regular work.[138]

III. WTO Involvement: Is There Really an International Consensus? "Pros and Cons."

The WTO Committee on Trade and Environment (CTE)[139] was created in order to provide a forum in which to examine the relationship between trade policies and the environment. Specifically, the CTE was charged to "... advise the WTO General Council on the need for changing WTO rules. It was the very first forum created within the WTO for 'making recommendations' on policy formulation in the area of trade and environment."[140] Despite this mandate, the CTE has proven weak because of its failure to actually alter any specific WTO. In order to change or alter a WTO agreement, the CTE has to first propose rules changes to the WTO's General Council. At this point, the General Council has to decide whether the proposal should be implemented.[141] Despite the existence of this procedure, the CTE has not recommended any changes to current trading rules.[142]

---

138 *See* WTO, *Doha Round*, http://www.wto.org/english/tratop_e/envir_e.htm (last accessed May 6, 2008).

139 The Website of the WTO provides the core information on "Trade and Environment."

> Sustainable development and protection and preservation of the environment are fundamental goals of the WTO. They are enshrined in the Marrakech Agreement, which established the WTO, and complement the WTO's objective to reduce trade barriers and eliminate discriminatory treatment in international trade relations. While there is no specific agreement dealing with the environment, under WTO rules members can adopt trade-related measures aimed at protecting the environment provided a number of conditions to avoid the misuse of such measures for protectionist ends are fulfilled.
>
> The WTO contributes to protection and preservation of the environment through its objective of trade openness, through its rules and enforcement mechanism, through work in different WTO bodies, and through ongoing efforts under the Doha Development Agenda. The Doha Agenda includes specific negotiations on trade and environment and some tasks assigned to the regular Trade and Environment Committee.

See WTO, *Trade and Development*, http://www.wto.org/english/tratop_e/envir_e.htm (last accessed May 6, 2008).

140 Huang & Labys, *supra* note 116.

141 *Id.*

142 *Id.*

Huang and Labys have noted that developing countries have shown a limited interest in pursuing environmental policies.[143] While Asian and Latin American countries have expressed some interest in an environmental agenda linking trade with the environment, African countries have to date not submitted a single proposal.[144] In their analysis, Huang and Labys discovered that the level of disengagement may result from a general lack of concern for environmental issues, or as more likely, from a variety of other reasons which reflect these nations' weak economic circumstances. Countries with limited prospects for attracting foreign direct investment may prefer to channel their negotiating resources into improving market access rather than in negotiating contentious environmental issues. Second, smaller developing nations may remain silent during negotiations so as to allow the "larger players" to take center stage in voicing their concerns about the incorporation of environmental standards that may be inimical to their economic growth. Third, some nations have voiced a more fundamental concern that WTO regulations concerning the environment and trade may be outside the scope of its power and mandate. Critics of imposing an environmental agenda on the WTO argue that the WTO is essentially a *trade organization* and thus, environmental issues should not be regulated through trade policies enforced by an international body like the WTO, but rather through domestic policies, legislation, or the treaty process adopted by individual nations.[145] These critics also aver that "trade experts" from the WTO who are charged with interpreting and enforcing trade rules have limited accountability to local or national governments, which

> ... gives the WTO undue power to rule on domestic regulations at the same time as its enforcement capacity has increased. These trends mark a shift in the understanding of the trade regime under the General Agreement on Tariffs and Trade (GATT), which ensured adequate room for domestic intervention in order to maintain economic and social stability.[146]

---

143 The analysis of developing nations' negotiating strategies has been adapted from Huang & Labys. *Id.*

144 *Id.*

145 *See, e.g.*, SURANOVIC, *supra* note 109, at 241.

146 *Id.* The General Agreement on Tariffs and Trade (GATT) was signed in 1947. The GATT was a multilateral agreement regulating trade among about 150 countries. The purpose of the GATT was the "substantial reduction of tariffs and other trade barriers and the elimination of preferences, on a reciprocal and mutually advantageous basis." *See GATT/WTO*, http://www.law.duke.edu/lib/researchguides/gatt.html (last accessed May 7, 2008).

There were eight *rounds* of negotiations under the GATT that addressed a myriad of trade issues. *See, e.g.*, ROBERT GILPIN, THE POLITICAL ECONOMY OF INTERNATIONAL RELATIONS 192 (1987) (discussing the original GATT negotiations in Geneva; the Annecy Round (1948-1949); the Torquay Round (1950-1951); the Geneva Round (1955-1956); the Dillon Round (1960-1962); the Kennedy Round

On the other side of the argument, those who favor environmental regulation through the intervention or aegis of the WTO argue that the WTO must provide a normalized mechanism for creating and then enforcing environmental standards. As Suranovic notes, if "environmental standards are included in the WTO framework then countries will have the option of taking countries who fail to implement agreed standards before the Dispute Settlement Body (DSB) for adjudication."[147] In essence, trade sanctions would be available to force countries to become compliant with environmental standards.[148]

(1964-1967); the Tokyo Round (1973-1979); and the Uruguay Round (1986-1994)). Prior to the creation of the WTO, the critical Uruguay Round of negotiations addressed issues such as tariffs, the inclusion of financial services in the trading rules, the trade related aspects of intellectual property (TRIPS Agreement), and the eventual inclusion of measures regulating international investments. As to agriculture, see GATT Press Summary, News of the Uruguay Round 8-11 (April 5, 1994); as to services, see Taunya L. McLarty, *Liberalized Telecommunications Trade in the WTO: Implications for the Universal Service Policy*, 51 FED. COMM. L.J. 20-33, 36, 38, 42-44 (1998); as to trade in financial services, see Mary E. Footer, *The International Regulation of Trade in Services Following Completion of the Uruguay Round*, 29 INT'L LAW 453, 465 (1995).

The Uruguay Round, which was completed on December 15, 1993 after seven years of negotiations, resulted in an agreement among 117 countries (including the U.S.) to reduce trade barriers and to create more comprehensive and enforceable world trade rules. The agreement, the *Final Act Embodying the Results of the Uruguay Round of Multilateral Trade Negotiations*, was signed in April 1994. The Uruguay Round agreement was approved and implemented by the U.S. Congress in December 1994, and went into effect on January 1, 1995. *See* Uruguay Round Trade Agreement, *Statement of Administrative Action, Agreement Establishing the World Trade Organization*, H.R. Doc. No. 316, 103d Cong., 2d Sess., Vol. 1, 659-667 (Sept. 27, 1994). *See also Worldtradelaw.net*, *at* http://library.duke.edu/metasearch/db/id/DUK00934.html (containing WTO negotiating history materials). This agreement also created the World Trade Organization (WTO), which came into being on January 1, 1995.

147 SURANOVIC, *supra* note 109, at 241.

148 *Id.* The Dispute Settlement Body is made up of all WTO member governments, usually represented by ambassadors or their equivalent rank. According to the website of the WTO:

> Settling disputes is the responsibility of the Dispute Settlement Body (the General Council in another guise), which consists of all WTO members. The Dispute Settlement Body has the sole authority to establish "panels" of experts to consider the case, and to accept or reject the panels' findings or the results of an appeal. It monitors the implementation of the rulings and recommendations, and has the power to authorize retaliation when a country does not comply with a ruling.

See Understanding the WTO: Settling Disputes,
http://www.wto.org/english/thewto_e/whatis_e/tif_e/disp1_e.htm (last accessed May 7, 2008).

The WTO encompasses a "stage" approach to dispute resolution and provides a procedure outlined in the following table:

There is, however, also an important negative viewpoint towards the inclusion of environmental standards within the WTO. Some environmentalists argue that the WTO approach should be abandoned altogether because, as a matter of philosophy and practice, sustainable development is simply incompatible with economic development. Dicken reports that many environmentalists are concerned that the "energy costs of transporting materials and goods across the world are not taken into account in setting prices of traded goods and that, in effect, trade is being massively subsidized at a huge short-term and long-term environmental cost,"[149] even though economic growth would raise resources for "objectives such as pollution abatement and the general protection of the environment."[150]

Opponents of the inclusion of environmental standards within the mandate of the WTO maintain that many developing countries are forced to choose between two main, and perhaps mutually exclusive, options: (1) attempt to compete successfully in the global market; or (2) embrace environmental standards. As such, opponents maintain that developing countries should make the policy choice to forego environmental standards in order to become competitive in the global market.[151] To support this

---

How long to settle a dispute?

These approximate periods for each stage of a dispute settlement procedure are target figures — the agreement is flexible. In addition, the countries can settle their dispute themselves at any stage. Totals are also approximate.

60 days	Consultations, mediation, etc
45 days	Panel set up and panelists appointed
6 months	Final panel report to parties
3 weeks	Final panel report to WTO members
60 days	Dispute Settlement Body adopts report (if no appeal)
Total = 1 year	**(without appeal)**
60-90 days	Appeals report
30 days	Dispute Settlement Body adopts appeals report
Total = 1y 3m	**(with appeal)**

Id. For a discussion of the weaknesses in dispute settlement procedures, see Raj Bhala, *Hegelian Reflections on Unilateral Action in the World Trading System*, 15 BERKELEY J. INT'L L. 159, 163-165 (1997).

149 DICKEN, *supra* note 112, at 597.

150 Huang & Labys, *supra* note 116,at 41 (indicating that studies show that international trade should help the environment because environmental indicators improve as income increases).

151 SURANOVIC, *supra* note 109, at 239.

argument, Huang and Labys note that there are studies that acknowledge that "pollution abatement policies reduce pollution and this decreases national income."[152] This position, of course, may be countered with the argument that the incorporation of environmental standards leads to an increase in "environmental goods"[153] and, to a large extent, "their impacts are not considered in national income account evaluations."[154] Additionally, "pollution abatement equipment can offset losses in industrial production due to more stringent environmental standards."[155]

IV. On Balance... An Argument for the Inclusion of Pollution Standards in the WTO Regime

So, which viewpoint is most correct? Several *policy questions* must be considered. Do environmental standards help or hinder international trade and development? Should the WTO be empowered to implement environmental standards? On balance, it appears that environmental standards should be implemented or at least prominently considered in trade agreements. The major argument in favor of such a proposition is that the long-term effects of incorporating environmental standards could lead to the creation of more jobs.[156] The OECD[157] maintains that there is a direct correlation between the environment and trade, arguing that "employment levels rise with pollution-control expenditures."[158] The OECD points to the experiences in such

---

152 Huang & Labys, *supra* note 116, at 3.

153 For a discussion of the concept of "environmental goods," see *Trade in Environmentally Preferable Goods and Services*, http://www.cec.org/programs_projects/trade_environ_econ/project/index.cfm?projectID=13&varl an=English (last accessed May 11, 2008) (testing the hypotheses whether liberalized rules under NAFTA serve to increase the use of environmentally preferable products).

154 *Id.*

155 *Id.*

156 *Id.* at 11.

157 OECD membership includes the following "high income" countries: Australia, Austria, Belgium, Canada, the Czech Republic, Denmark, Finland, France, Germany, Greece, Hungary, Iceland, Ireland, Italy, Japan, Korea, Luxembourg, Mexico, Netherlands, New Zealand, Norway, Poland, Portugal, Slovak Republic, Spain, Sweden, Switzerland, Turkey, United Kingdom, and the United States.

According to the website of the organization, "The OECD brings together the governments of countries committed to democracy and the market economy from around the world to: Support sustainable economic growth; boost employment; raise living standards; maintain financial stability; assist other countries' economic development; and contribute to growth in world trade."

See http://www.oecd.org (the website of the OECD) (last visited May 7, 2008). Note the preeminent position of "sustainable development" as a core objective of the organization.

158 Huang & Labys, *supra* note 116, at 11.

countries as the United States, France, and Norway[159] and the clear connection of environmental considerations with the growth of productivity. Huang and Labys cite the United States Environmental Protection Agency which maintains that "environmental policies induce 'more cost-effective processes that reduce both emissions and the overall cost of doing business.'"[160] Of course, this represents the viewpoint of the developed world.

Second, the WTO must take on frontally anti-environmental incorporation arguments raised by developing nations concerning "market access." One such argument deals with the issue of protection under the guise of environmental protection. "Under the guise of environmental policies, foreign products might be prohibited from access to markets where domestic products are more expensive."[161] Thus, the inclusion of standards such as "auto emissions, agricultural regulations controlling pesticide residue, or product component quality, have been criticized by trading countries that believe these policies are designed to restrict market access for foreign products under the guise of insuring food safety or promoting cleaner air."[162] In order to counter, or at least neutralize this argument, environmentalists have to pressure governments to adopt reasonable international standards that will be applicable to all WTO member nations and will guard against the adoption of unilateralism on the part of WTO member states. Huang and Labys note: "Due to the absence of an effective international enforcement mechanism, some countries have to resort to unilateral actions. Under most circumstances, unilateral actions are a violation of existing WTO jurisprudence."[163]

Third, although the relationship between the environment and trade may be in dispute, there is no doubt that there is a close relationship between trade and the global business environment. Kenichi Ohmae, the Japanese management guru, coined the phrase "borderless world." Much of our understanding about globalization comes from the writings and research of Professor Ohmae. His formulation, termed the *Five Stages of Globalization*, indicate the strong correlation between international trade and globalization. Each of the five stages involves significant issues relating to international trade and many, if not all, contain environmental aspects. According to Professor Ohmae, an international business enters the international business environment through a progression of activities that can generally be described as:

1. Exporting, using the distribution system of a business found in the host country;
2. Exporting, setting up a distribution system in the host country;

---

159 *Id.*

160 *Id.* at 12.

161 *Id.* at 28.

162 *Id.*

163 *Id.* at 28-29.

3. Manufacturing and distributing products in the host country—but maintaining a company's ties with its "home" country, perhaps by acting as a subsidiary corporation or entity of the *parent* company;
4. Insiderization, becoming like any other manufacturing concern located in the host country—acquiring the identity of a national company or entity;
5. Becoming a fully globalized company—operating in many host countries simultaneously; where it may be difficult to ascertain the country to which a fully globalized company is attached.[164]

In this context, for example, it is important once again to examine the arguments of Professors Huang and Labys. They note, as an example, that "fuel efficient cars not only reduce air emissions in the United States but also force U.S. manufacturers to develop more fuel-efficient models." Thus, international trade is literally shaping the agendas of world economies by "intensifying the environmental impacts of domestic production by expanding international markets." International trade enables countries to obtain desired products from their trading partners "that are domestically either unavailable or protected by strict laws and hence effectively pass the environmental effects of consumption" to other countries. Because national policies regarding standards are often attacked as just another form of protectionism, "efforts to restore environmental quality within countries and to protect the global commons… are erroneously misguided."[165]

Because the arguments on both sides of the issue are convincing and reflect very different policy perspectives, there may not be a clear and direct answer to the conundrum. However, the reality is that trade agreements certainly impact the environment. Although the WTO may not be "the only game in town," it is certainly *a* major player on the world scene. Thus, the WTO may be a starting point for at least eliminating the tension—real or imagined—between the global business environment, international trade, and core environmental concerns.

---

[164] *See, e.g.*, KENICHI OHMAE, THE NEXT GLOBAL STAGE: THE CHALLENGES AND OPPORTUNITIES IN OUR BORDERLESS WORLD (2005).

[165] Adapted from Huang & Labys, *supra* note 12, at 40-41.

CHAPTER 6

DILEMMAS IN INTERNATIONAL MARKETING AND LAW: PRIVACY AND COMPETITIVENESS IN THE AGE OF GOOGLE

By
Héctor R. Lozada

In the age of Google, when everything you say is forever searchable, the future belongs to those who leave no footprints.

Thomas Friedman
The New York Times, July, 16, 2010

1. What Lies Ahead

Without debate, the Internet has been one of the most significant accomplishments of the Twentieth Century, one that presently affects not only the way we interact with business organizations in the Twenty-first Century, but how we interact with one another. There is no doubt that in the future, international trade will utilize the Internet as a main portal of its commerce. Consider the following: as of July 2010, twenty countries, including China, the United States and Russia, account for about 77 percent of all world Internet users, leaving 226 countries accounting for about 23 percent of Internet use.[166] Fifty eight countries have high Internet penetration rates, that is, fifty percent or more of the population in each country is using the Internet.[167] China and Russia's rate of growth in Internet users for the period 2000-2010 is over 1,000 percent, each, while the U.S.'s growth is 146 percent. While the percent of the population with access to the Internet is 76 percent in the United States, it is 43 percent and 29 percent in Russia and China, respectively, leaving an enormous potential for growth. Yet, with only less than a third of its population having access to the Internet, China still represents the largest world user, followed by the United States.

As a result, businesses and governments (especially politicians) are more interested than ever in tracking Internet use. For example, Nielsen Online reports that global Internet users spend 38 hours per month, on average, on their personal computers, and one hour surfing the web (also on average), resulting in visits to about 1,600 per

---

166 Internet World Statistics, *Top 20 Countries with Highest Number of Internet Users*, at http://www.internetworldstats.com/top20.htm (last visited July 15, 2010).

167 Internet World Statistics, *Top 58 Countries with the Highest Internet Penetration Rate*, at http://www.internetworldstats.com/top25.htm (last visited July 15, 2010).

person per month.[168] Additionally, it is possible to track the flow of data around the world. Internet Traffic Report reports on a world map the speed and reliability of connections, by world region, through an index between zero and 100 (the higher the index, the faster and more reliable the connection in that region).[169]

If the above were not enough reason to give anyone pause, reflect on the following: Cisco Systems, disclosed in June 2009 the results of a study that confirms consumer broadband usage and global IP network traffic continues to climb at an overwhelming pace due to new forms and expanded usage of interactive media, and the explosion of video content across multiple devices. The study projects that global IP traffic will increase fivefold by 2013.[170]

A major player is Google.com, the Internet services company whose value as a global brand grew from 2008 to 2009 by 25 percent to almost $32 billion.[171] In this article, we explore the issues that are arising regarding privacy, consumer trust, competitive actions and potential monopolistic practices of this company as it expands its global reach. We also provide remarks at the end regarding the issues that we will confront as new media intermingles with companies like Google—who will be major sources of consumer and business information relating to international trade.

2. **Organic Search Engines**

Because the large amount of data that now exists virtually in cyberspace, *search engines* are critical elements of Internet use is. A search engine is designed to seek out for information on the World Wide Web. The results of the search are usually presented in a list of "hits." The hits may consist of web pages, images, information and other types of files. Some search engines also mine data (that is, extract patterns from data) available in databases or open directories. Unlike Web directories, which are maintained by human editors, search engines operate algorithmically or are a mixture of algorithmic and human input.

Yahoo.com, created in 1994, was one of the first search engines and quickly became very popular by just providing a list of the creators' (Jerry Yang and David Filo) favorite web sites.[172] Its popularity, however, has been eclipsed by Google.com, which

---

168 *Nielsen Online Global Index Chart*, http://www.nielsen-online.com/resources.jsp?section=pr_netv (last visited July 15, 2010).

169 *Internet Traffic Report*, at http://www.internettrafficreport.com/ (last visited July 15, 2010).

170 "New Cisco Visual Networking Index Forecasts Global IP Traffic to Increase Fivefold by 2013," http://newsroom.cisco.com/dlls/2009/prod_060909.html (last visited July 15, 2010).

171 Interbrand (2009), "Best Global Brands 2009," *available at* http://www.interbrand.com/best_global_brands.aspx (last visited July 19, 2010).

172 Lee Underwood (2004), "A Brief History of Search Engines," *available at* http://www.webreference.com/authoring/search_history/ (last visited July 15, 2010).

was launched in 1997. Google is a play on the word "googol," a mathematical term for the number represented by the numeral 1 followed by 100 zeros, which the company claims is a reflection of their mission to organize a seemingly infinite amount of information on the web.[173] According to Peter Hidas of the Gartner Group, "Google runs over one million servers in data centers around the world and processes over one billion search requests and twenty petabytes[174] of user-generated data every day.[175] Hidas also states that "ninety-nine percent of Google's revenue is derived from its advertising programs. For the year 2009, Google reported $22.9 billion in advertising revenues[176]

3. Before Going Global, A Local Example: New Jersey and Online Privacy

The Internet has become one of the most powerful business tools today. Much like a telephone, users conduct transactions over the Internet. With advancements in technology especially in regards to ad customization, privacy comes into question. Businesses through the Internet identify and categorize their customers. This information allows marketers to customize ads to users based on personal information. Storing personal information is also how companies use direct marketing.[177] Prior purchase behavior leads them to advertise products similar to previous purchases. While consumers like to see products that fit their needs, how far should marketers be allowed to go? Is it an invasion of privacy if marketers are able to use facial recognition technology to recognize and differentiate between consumers in the same household? This technology has the potential to allow marketers to distinguish when a father is at the computer on-line as opposed to his teenage son. Marketers would then customize ads depending on the user, showing the father advertisements about retirement or other things specific to his interests. His son on the other hand would see ads about video games, college scholarships, etc.

On April 22, 2008 New Jersey became the first court in the nation to rule that people have an expectation of privacy when online.[178] When ruling in state cases, this new ruling will take precedent of the much weaker Supreme Court decisions stating there is no privacy on the internet.[179] This ruling was handed down in a case involving federal officials seeking a user's private information during the investigation of a crime involving her computer. The seven-member court ruled that federal officials do have a

---

173 http://www.google.com/corporate/history.html (last visited July 15, 2010).

174 A *petabyte* is a unit of information equal to one quadrillion bytes. *See* http://www.techterms.com.

175 "Google: one million servers and counting,"*Pandia Search Engine News*, July 2, 2007, *available at* http://www.pandia.com/sew/481-gartner.html (last visited July 18, 2010).

176 *See* http://investor.google.com/financial/2009/tables.html (last visited July 15, 2010).

177 Privacy Rights Clearinghouse. *Privacy in Cyyberspace, available at* http://www.privacyrights.org/fs/fs18-cyb.htm#Marketing (Last visited July 15, 2010).

178 Tom Hester, "NJ justices call e-privacy surfers' right," STAR LEDGER April 22, 2008 Front Cover.

179 *Id.*

right to a user's information when investigating a crime but they must follow legal procedures, securing a grand jury warrant first. Grayson Barber, a Trenton-based lawyer arguing for privacy groups explained that "people use the internet much like the phone making personal and sometimes sensitive transactions they don't believe police will be able to access."[180] The court's ruling, "We now hold that citizens have a reasonable expectation of privacy protected by Article I ... of the New Jersey Constitution, in the subscriber information they provide to Internet service providers -- just as New Jersey citizens have a privacy interest in their bank records stored by banks and telephone billing records kept by phone companies"[181] seems to lend itself to a broader interpretation. New Jersey's ruling means that the court interprets New Jersey's constitution to say that ordinary state citizens have a fundamental expectation of privacy when online.[182]

The ruling in New Jersey could be a starting point for controlling privacy on the Internet. New Jersey's court has recognized that people have a right to privacy online similarly to the telephone. If more states follow suit, the beginnings of privacy laws regarding the Internet could be formed proactively preventing issues involving technology such as facial recognition.

4. Back to the Global Arena: China, Russia and the U.S.

Since 2008, there is a growing issue regarding the intentions of the Chinese who are proactively attempting to limit access to the Internet on "policy" grounds, eerily similar to the rationale offered in Burstyn. The implications are truly staggering as there are reports that there are as many as 300 million Chinese Internet users and Internet use is on the rise. Interestingly, in June 2009, the Chinese government accused Google's English-language world-wide search engine of spreading "vulgar content" (recall the "sacrilegious" standard proffered in Burstyn) and indicated that the Chinese government had carried out "punishment measures." Malcolm Moore has raised concerns about the Chinese action and indicated that Google had been repeatedly blocked in China for actions that were "upsetting to the regime." The first actions occurred as early as 2002. In blocking Google, an official from the Chinese Foreign Ministry stated: "I want to stress that Google China is a company operating within China to provide Internet search services and it should strictly abide by Chinese laws and regulations." The government essentially accused Google of "spreading pornography"—although the article speculated that the "block could be linked to competition with the Chinese internet search engine, Baidu." Jeremy Goldkorn, the founder of Danwei, a website that analyzes the Chinese media, indicated that the order to ban Google "had probably been vaguely communicated to [i]nternet companies" in China.

---

[180] *Id.*

[181] *Id.*

[182] *Id.*

Further, Saul Hansell has observed that the Obama administration, through the actions of Gary Locke, U.S. Commerce Secretary, and Ron Kirk, the U.S. Trade Representative, had immediately lodged a formal protest with the Chinese government over its plans to require that all computers in China be equipped with computer software that would block access to certain websites. The Chinese government maintained that filtering software, known as Green Dam-Youth Escort, was designed to block pornography and other "unhealthy information." In rejecting the Chinese contentions, Kirk noted: "Protecting children from inappropriate content is a legitimate objective, but this is an inappropriate means that is likely to have a broader scope"—raising the larger question "whether the software would lead to more censorship of the Internet in China."[183] Loretta Chao, of the Wall Street Journal, noted that "The software, which the government says was designed to filter out pornography and other contents inappropriate for children, ... [seems] to be capable of filtering political content as well. It would add an extra layer to China's wide-reaching methods of regulating Internet use."[184] The ban, introduced at short notice, was also challenged on grounds that it might violate World Trade Organization rules because companies, such as Hewlett-Packard Co., a U.S. corporation, and Dell Inc.-Lenovo Group Ltd. of China, were given only six weeks' notice to comply with its terms.

Ironically, an American firm, Solid Oak Software, claims that Green Dam includes stolen copyrighted code from one of its proprietary products, and has launched legal action.[185] Experts quoted in the article stressed the more nefarious interpretation of the ban, rejecting the Chinese contention that Green Dam was designed to protect young people from "unhealthy" and "poisonous" pornographic and violent content, and instead noting that "Michigan experts found that it also scans text for 'politically sensitive' phrases."[186]

In January, 2010, Google's conflict with China escalated.[187] At the time, the company was claiming it was tired of dealing with China's censorship and was annoyed with its hackers. Google decided to end its four-year practice of omitting search results that the Chinese government considered subversive or pornographic after blaming Chinese computer hackers for an attack it said was aimed at stealing the company's technology and e-mail information from human rights activists.[188] Beginning in March,

---

[183] *See* Saul Hansell, "U.S. asks China to rescind edict requiring Web filters," INTERNATIONAL HERALD TRIBUNE, June 24, 2009, at A6, *available at* http://www.nytimes.com/2009/06/25/world/asia/25censor.html.

[184] Loretta Chao, "U.S. urges China to revoke PC software rule; Beijing's order to pre-install Web filters on computers set to take effect on July 1[2009]," GLOBE AND MAIL (Toronto), June 25, 2009, at B11.

[185] *See* "Dammed if you do," ECONOMIST, June 27, 2009, at 49.

[186] *Id.*

[187] *See* Daniel Indiviglio, "A cowardly decision," USA TODAY. Jan 15, 2010. pg. A.12.

[188] *See* Tini Tran, "China renews Google's operating license," ASSOCIATED PRESS, July 11, 2010, *available at*

2010, Google started to automatically reroute search requests from the mainland to its Hong Kong service. Search requests at Google.cn from within mainland China require an extra click that then takes the user to the Hong Kong site, which isn't subject to Beijing's censorship rules. That small concession was enough to persuade China's regulators to renew the license in July, 2010.[189] As a side note, while the conflict with China was escalating, Google had to try to contain quickly mounting criticism of Buzz, its social network, apologizing to users for features that were widely seen as endangering privacy in the U.S.[190] After disengaging the features that were of concern to privacy advocates, the issue lost steam.[191]

Beyond China's position on the fundamental right of nations to require filters in search engines like Google or Bing, the growing threat of cyberwar attacks that could wreak havoc on computer systems and the Internet has presently resulted in a heated dispute between Russia and the United States. Russia is proposing an international treaty similar to the one negotiated for chemical weapons and has pressed for this approach while the United States argues that a treaty is unnecessary, pushing instead for improved cooperation among international law enforcement groups.[192] Over the July 4, 2009 weekend an Internet denial-of-service attack aimed at 27 American and South Korean government agencies and commercial websites jammed more than a third of them for a period of at least five days.[193] South Korean officials proceeded to accuse North Korean military or intelligence agents of being responsible for the attack in retaliation for new United Nations sanctions. John Markoff of the *New York Times* reports that "[C]yberwarfare specialists cautioned. . . that the Internet was effectively a "wilderness of mirrors," and that attributing the source of cyberattacks and other kinds of exploitation is difficult at best and sometimes impossible."[194]

---

http://www.google.com/hostednews/ap/article/ALeqM5gKrY51vO2V86xiICf35Q05J0FIEAD9GSQSR00 (last visited July 19, 2010).

[189] *Id.*

[190] *See* Miguel Helft, "Anger Leads To Apology From Google About Buzz," N. Y. TIMES. Feb 15, 2010. pg. B.3.

[191] *Id.*

[192] *See* John Markoff & Andrew E. Kramer "U.S. and Russia Differ on a Treaty for Cyberspace," N.Y. TIMES, June 28, 2009 at A1, *available at* http://www.nytimes.com/2009/06/28/world/28cyber.html?_r=1&scp=1&sq=russia%20and%20internet&st=cse.

[193] *See* Choe Sang-Hun & John Markoff "Cyberattacks Jam Government and Commercial Web Sites in U.S. and South Korea," N.Y. TIMES, July 9, 2009 at A4, *available at* http://www.nytimes.com/2009/07/09/technology/09cyber.html?scp=2&sq=Cyberattacks%20Jam%20Government%20and%20Commercial%20Web%20Sites%20in&st=Search

[194] *See* John Markoff "Internet's Anonymity Makes Cyberattack Hard to Trace," N.Y. TIMES, July 17, 2009 at A5, *available at* http://www.nytimes.com/2009/07/17/technology/17cyber.html?scp=1&sq=Cyberattacks%20Jam%20Government%20and%20Commercial%20Web%20Sites%20in&st=Search

The policy debate in Washington D.C. has intensified as a result. In December, 2009, the United States began talks with Russia and a United Nations arms control committee about strengthening Internet security and limiting military use of cyberspace.[195] By April 2010, John Markoff reported that there are signs of agreement between the U.S. and Russia regarding what would be considered the most important step in combating Internet crime: doing away with the anonymity that has long been a central tenet of Internet culture.[196] Markoff reports that both Col. Gen. Boris N. Miroshnikov, an official with the Russian Interior Ministry, and Stewart A. Baker, a fellow at the Center for Strategic and International Studies in Washington, and the former chief counsel for the National Security Agency both agreed in a panel presentation that the fundamental problem that nations face in cyberspace is anonymity, which in their view gives criminals permission to act.[197] At the time of this writing, these negotiations continue.

5. Meanwhile... in The European Union

In late 2009, Google was at the center of a major controversy in Italy. Italian prosecutors argued that Google was negligent because it allowed a video of high school kids bullying a disabled classmate to stay on its Italian-language video service for two months in 2006. The company responded that it removed the video several hours after being alerted of its existence.[198] At stake for Google was that if prosecutors were able to persuade the judge that the company knew the video was online and chose to do nothing, Google might be forced to change its operating practices in Italy and the rest of Europe by creating filters to flag offensive videos. This case decided on February 24, 2010. In a decision that for the first time held company executives as criminally responsible for content posted online via their system, the judge convicted three Google executives of violating Italian privacy laws.[199] The verdict, which the company emphatically and

---

[195] *See* John Markoff & Andrew E. Kramer, "In Shift, U.S. Talks to Russia on Internet Security," N.Y. TIMES, December 13, 2009 *available at* http://www.nytimes.com/2009/12/13/science/13cyber.html?_r=1&scp=1&sq=Russia%20and%20cyberterrorism&st=cse.

[196] *See* John Markoff, "At Internet Conference, Signs of Agreement Appear Between U.S. and Russia," N.Y. TIMES, April 16, 2010 at A14, *available at* http://www.nytimes.com/2010/04/16/science/16cyber.html?scp=5&sq=cyberterrorism&st=cse.

[197] *Id.*

[198] *See* Eric Sylvers, "Prosecutors Press Case Against Google in Italy," N.Y. TIMES, NOVEMBER 25, 2009 *available at* http://www.nytimes.com/2009/11/26/technology/companies/26video.html?scp=1&sq=Google%20and%20Italy&st=Search .

[199] *See* Rachel Donadio, "Larger Threat Is Seen in Google Case," N.Y. TIMES, February 25, 2010 at A1, *available at* http://www.nytimes.com/2010/02/25/technology/companies/25google.html?scp=1&sq=google%20executives%20convicted%20in%20italy&st=Search.

angrily vowed to appeal,[200] could have far-reaching implications worldwide for Internet users and providers. The conviction seems to indicate that Google is not simply a tool for its users, as it contends, but is effectively no different from any other media company, like newspapers or television, that provides content and could be regulated.[201] One of the three executives, Google's global privacy counsel, Peter Fleischer stated that the company is deeply troubled by this decision, and, further, "[i]f company employees like me can be held criminally liable for any video on a hosting platform, when they had absolutely nothing to do with the video in question, then our liability is unlimited."[202]

The ruling in Italy came at a time when the business environment for Google in Europe is turning more and more complicated due to a wave of antitrust complaints. Take for example the French Competition Authority. In early July, 2010, the French authority officially declared Google a monopoly in a decision that appears to go beyond any previous official ruling in the United States or elsewhere.[203] The authority concluded that Google holds a dominant position on the advertising market related to online searches, and its search engine is widely popular, accounting for about 90 percent of Web searches made in France. Having determined Google has a monopoly, the agency ordered the company to resume offering its services to a French company called Navx, which sells a database to let drivers know where the French police are likely to have radar traps in operation. Google stopped selling advertising space to Navx's because it considered its business distasteful and they did not want to potentially assist Navx's customers to use the product to help them act illegally.[204] When Google stopped doing business with Navx in November, 2009, those using search terms like "radar trap" in French could no longer learn of the company's product and, a few clicks later, buy it. This prompted a complaint to the French government from Navx in February, 2010, in which the company states that its sales had plunged and that as a result it was facing problems raising capital.[205]

In its decision, the French authority ordered Google to resume selling ads to Navx and to produce clear policies on when advertisers would be turned down. It also came down hard on the company by stating that discriminatory practices may harm competition when customers of a company holding a dominant position find themselves

---

200 *See* John Hooper, "Google executives convicted in Italy over abuse video," The Guardian, February 24, 2010, *available at* http://www.guardian.co.uk/technology/2010/feb/24/google-video-italy-privacy-convictions.

201 *See supra* note 199.

202 *Id.*

203 *See* Floyd Norris, "France Calls Google a Monopoly," N.Y. TIMES, July 2, 2010 at B1, *available at* http://www.nytimes.com/2010/07/02/business/02norris.html?emc=eta1.

204 *Id.*

205 *See* "Navx Files Complaint With the French Competition Authority Against Google," *available at* http://blog.taragana.com/pr/navx-files-complaint-with-the-french-competition-authority-against-google-13445/ (last visited July 21, 2010).

disadvantaged in the competition on their own market.[206] Google found this finding troubling, particularly since Navx is not one of its competitors. Google's position, rejected by the French, is that the relevant market is all of advertising, in which Google has a tiny share, rather than online search ads, in which it is dominant. It appears that if the French authorities do not reverse that conclusion in their final ruling, it will be the first official precedent in Europe rejecting Google's argument.

6. Final Thoughts

International trade has undergone a wholesale revolution because of the growth in the use of the Internet by both sellers and buyers. The growing use of search engines to navigate the Internet, the evolution of smartphones that allow individuals access to the Internet wherever they are (via browsers or third-party apps), and the success of social media sites like Facebook.com have afforded us some major opportunities for businesses, but these do not come without major challenges. Social media gives people today the sense of community and closeness. Unfortunately with new social media, an argument can be made that a person's privacy can start to diminish. The Internet is one of the best tools in which marketers track customer buying behavior patterns for a company. Unfortunately this can sometimes affect people's privacy. According to Steve Lohr,[207] Congress and the Federal Trade Commission are mulling tighter restrictions on online data collection, disclosure and use. A group of privacy groups sent their principles for controlling data collection and use, in a letter sent to members of Congress on Monday, April 26, 2010. The groups include the Center for Digital Democracy, the Consumer Federation of America, the Electronic Frontier Foundation, the United States Public Interest Research Group and the World Privacy Forum. Their suggested steps include limiting the ability of web sites and ad networks to use behavioral data to 24 hours after it is collected, and requiring consumers' permission — an opt-in approach — to hold such data beyond 24 hours.[208] In addition these privacy advocacy groups say that people should be aware and informed about who is tracking their web browsing patterns and that individuals should have the option to remove their personal data from the tracker's database.

As the above was being discussed, Apple introduced the iPad, its version of a tablet computer that was initially marketed as an e-reader, but is presently talked about as a content consuming device.[209] After a very successful launch in late April, 2010, by

---

[206] *See supra* note 199.

[207] *See* Lohr, Steve 2010. "Privacy Concerns Limit Online Ads". http://bits.blogs.nytimes.com/2010/04/30/privacy-concerns-limit-online-ads-study-says/, (last visited July 21, 2010).

[208] *Id.*

[209] *See* Mark Lindler, "Is the iPad a consumption only device?" *available at* http://marklindner.info/blog/2010/03/28/is-the-ipad-a-consumption-only-device/ (last visited July 21, 2010).

early June, 2010, the company was dealing with a hacking incident in which prominent users of Apple's new iPad 3G, including military and government officials as well as media personalities and celebrities, had their e-mail addresses hacked by a group that shared its findings with online publication Valleywag to point out security flaws in AT&T's Web servers.[210] Even Apple, who boasts superior security in its products, was susceptible to an attack via its Internet service provider, re-emphasizing concerns over privacy.

As a conclusion, we ask "Where now?" As more and more people gain access to the Internet, the issue of privacy will continue to be on the forefront. What may companies do/do not with the information that they gather from customers via web-based transactions? What about governments? Should they be allowed to keep private information of their citizens online forever? As new technologies surface, for example face recognition technology, should companies be entitled to match faces with the personal and behavioral information that they presently collect via web-transactions? If more and more of our economic activity becomes web-based or web-oriented, are we not more susceptible to cyberterrorism attacks that could seriously harm not only a country's economy, but the global economy? Regulations need to be set now before the technology is fully developed so that ground rules are set so that we may reap the benefits of the new technologies without individuals, governments and organizations feeling like their privacy has been invaded and personal or private information taken without permission. But, who? How? It seems to be country by country, or even state by states as in the U.S., but eventually, should we not aim at global consensus?

What is certain is that international trade has been inextricably connected to the Internet. As trade volume increases through the use of Internet sites, the nature of issues will change but the importance of the Internet as a major driver of international trade certainly will not diminish.

[210] Suzanne Choney, "iPad 3G Owners' E-Mail Addresses Hacked," June 9, 2010, *available at* http://www.msnbc.msn.com/id/37602751/ns/technology_and_science-tech_and_gadgets/ (Last visited July 22, 2010). The hacker was arrested on June 15, 2010 on drug possession charges.

BIBLIOGRAPHIC REFERENCES

CHAPTER 1

Aguilar, Linda M. (1992). "NAFTA: A Review of the Issues," *Economic Perspectives* (Federal Reserve Bank of Chicago), pp. 12-19.

Annex 1C of the Marrakesh Agreement Establishing the World Trade Organization, signed in Marrakesh, Morocco on 15 April 1994.

Barber, Edwin I. (1982). "Investment-Trade Nexus," in *U.S. International Economic Policy* (Gary Clyde Hufbauer, ed.) (Institute for International Economics).

Becker, Elizabeth. (2004). "U.S. Will Cut Farm Subsidies in Trade Deal," *The New York Times* (on line), at http://www.nytimes.com/2004/07/31/business/worldbusiness/31geneva.html, July 31.

Bergiel, Blaise J. & Erich B. Bergiel. (1999). "Country-of-Origin as a Surrogate Indicator: Implications/Strategies," *Global Competitiveness*, Vol. 7, pp. 187-195.

Bhala, Raj. (1995). "Rethinking Antidumping Law," *George Washington Journal of International Law and Economics*, Vol. 29, pp. 1-144, abstracted in Raj Bhala, *International Trade Law: Theory and Practice* (LexisNexis, 2d ed.), pp. 830-839.

Bhala, Raj. (2001). *International Trade Law: Theory and Practice* (Lexis Nexis, 2d ed.).

Bhala, Raj. (2002). "The Development of the GATT-WTO System and Its Relationship With China," in Raj Bhala, *International Trade Law: Theory and Practice* (LexisNexis, 2d ed.), pp. 127-141.

Czinkota, Michael R., Ilkka A. Ronkainen, Michael H. Moffett & Eugene O. Moynihan. (2001). *Global Business* (Dryden).

Dam, Kenneth W. (1970). *The GATT* (Southwestern, 3rd ed.).

Daniels, John, Lee H. Radebaugh & Daniel Sullivan. (2007). "Theories and Institutions: Trade and Investment," in *International Business* (Pearson), pp. 200-203.

Department of the Treasury. (1991). "Harmonized Trade Schedule of the United States Code of Federal Regulations No. 19, Customs Duties, Importing into the United States."

Economist. (2010). "Fading Trading," January 30, p. 85.

Gilpin, Robert. (1987). *The Political Economy of International Relations* (Princeton University Press).

House of Representatives. (1994). "Statement of Administrative Action, Agreement on Trade-Related Aspects of Intellectual Property Rights," September 27.

House Committee on Ways and Means. (1997). "Overview and Compilation of U.S. Trade Statute," June 25.

Magnier, Mark. (1999). "Blockades to Food Exports Hide Behind Invisible Shields," *The Journal of Commerce* (on line), Vol. 18.

World Trade Organization. (2010). "An Introduction to the WTO," at http://www.wto.org.

World Trade Organization. (2010). "Dispute Settlement," at http://www.wto.org/english/tratop_e/dispu_e/dispu_e.htm.

Yip, George S. (2003). *Total Global Strategy II* (Prentice Hall, 3rd ed.).

CHAPTER 2

Ager, Brian. (2003). "Compulsory Licensing Is Not The Answer," at http://www.managingip.com.

AIDS.org. (2007). "Compulsory Licensing for Bridging the Gap—Treatment Access in Developing Countries" [Interview with James Love], at http://www.aids.org/atn/a-314-01.html.

Alcorn, Keith. (2007). "Brazil Issues Compulsory License on Efavirenz" [*Aidsmap News*], at http://www.aidsmap.com/en/news/0550CE62-3F90-4603-932C-EF69E1B4485D.asp.

Canadian HIV/AIDS Legal Network. (2006). "The Jean Chrétien Pledge to Africa Act and It's Impact on Improving Access to HIV/AIDS Treatment in Developing Countries," at http://library.catie.ca/PDF/P37/23751.pdf.

Choudhary, Sanjeev & Khomba Singh. (2008). "Govt. may use compulsory licensing for drug companies only in emergency," *The Economic Times,* at http://economictimes.indiatimes.com/articleshow/2921237.cms, April 3.

Dutfield, Graham. (2008). "Delivering Drugs to the Poor: Will the TRIPS Amendment Help? *American Journal of Law and Medicine*, Vol. 34, pp. 107-124.

Finston, Susan. (2008). "Compulsory Licensing in Thailand: Reality Bites" [*PolicyBytes.org.*], at http://www.policybytes.org/blog/policybytes.nsf/dx/compulsory-licensing-in-thailand-reality-bites.htm, September 12.

Kim, Do Hyung. (2007). "Research Guide on TRIPS and Compulsory Licensing: Access to Innovative Pharmaceuticals for Least Developed Countries," *NYU Law Global,* at http://www.nyulawglobal.org/globalex/TRIPS_Compulsory_Licensing.htm.

Oxfam International. (2007). "Patents versus Patients: Five years after the Doha Declaration," at http://www.oxfam.org.uk/what_we_do/issues/health/downloads/bp95_patents.pd No. 14, pp. 1-36.

People's Daily Online. (2007). "MSF rallies support for Thailand's compulsory licensing on AIDS drugs," at http://english.peopledaily.com.cn/200702/03/eng20070203_347301.html, February 3.

PhRMA. (2009). "Healthcare in the Developing World [FAQs]," at http://world.phrma.org/faq.html.

Sands, Katharine W. (2006). "Prescription drugs: India Values their compulsory licensing provision—should the United States follow in India's footsteps?" *Houston Journal of International Law* [digital], at http://www.entrepreneur.com/tradejournals/article/157099525.html.

Singh, Someshwar. (1999). "Compulsory Licensing Good For US Public, Not Others," at http://www.twnside.org.sg/title/public-cn.htm, October 29.

World Trade Organization. (2005). "Press Release: Members OK amendment to make health flexibility permanent," at http://www.wto.org/english/news_e/pres05_e/pr426_e.htm, December 6.

CHAPTER 3

American Society of Quality. (2008). "Importers Share Responsibility for Unsafe Products," *Business Wire*, at www.asq.org/media-room/press-releases/2008/20080110-importers-share-responsibility.html, January 9.
Associated Press. (2007). "Chinese economy slows to sizzling 11.5% growth," at http://www.usatoday.com/money/world/2007-10-25-china-gdp_N.htm, October 25.
Associated Press/Reuters. (2009). "2 face execution over China milk scandal," www.msnbc.msn.com/id/28787126, January 22.
Barboza, David. (2007). "When fakery turns fatal," *New York Times*, June 5, p. C1.
Barboza, David. (2007). "China Finds Poor Quality In Its Stores," *International Herald Tribune*, at www.iht.com/articles/2007/07/05/business/05safety.php, July 5.
Basker, Emek & Pham Hoang Van. (2009). "Wal-Mart as Catalyst to U.S.-China Trade," at http://ideas.repec.org/p/umc/wpaper/o710.html.
Bassolino, Francis. (2008). "Sourcing from China: You get what you pay for," *Multichannel Merchant*, at www.multichannelmerchant.com/opsandfulfillment/archive/index3.html, April 1.
Blanchard, David & Jorge Perez Izquierdo. (2007). "Taming the Dragon," *Industry Week*, November.
Blodgett, Mark, Richard J. Hunter, Jr. & Robert M. Hayden. (2009). "Foreign Direct Investment, Trade, and China's Competition Laws," *Denver Journal of Environmental Law and Policy,* Vol. 37, No. 2, pp. 201-231.
Canaves, Sky & Juliet Ye. (2008). "Chinese parents file milk lawsuit; couple's claim comes as officials oppose litigation," *Wall Street Journal*, p. A21, at www.online.wsj.com/article/SB122279824170891107.html, October 1.
Central Intelligence Agency. (2009/2010). *World Factbook*, at https://www.cia.gov/library/publications/the-worldfactbook/rankorder/2007rank.html.
Chao, Loretta. (2009). "Infant Illnesses Force Major Chinese Baby-Formula Recall; Kidney-Stone Cases Raise Questions on Product Safety," *Wall Street Journal*, p. A8, at www.online.wsj.com/article/SB122122542993527897.html, September 13.
Charnley, Stephen. (2008). "Great Wall No Longer," *Canadian Underwriter*, March.
China Daily. (2009). "China can achieve 8% GDP growth through efforts," at http://www.chinadaily.com.cn/bizchina/2009-03/02/content_7527011.htm, March 2.
D'Amico, Esther. (2007). "China: Flagging Up Quality Controls," *Chemical Week,* Vol. 169, at www.glgroup.com/NewsWatchPrefs/Print.aspx?pid=16647, September.
DeWoskin, Ken. (2007). "The 'Made in China' Stigma Shock," *Far Eastern Economic Review*, Vol. 170, pp. 9-13.
Economist Intelligence Unit (2007). "Stoking Protectionism," p.1, at www.economist.com, August 16.
Fairclough, Gordon. (2007). "China-Product Scare Hits Home, Too; Exports of Toxic

Toothpaste Halted, But Government Lets Domestic Sales Go On," *Wall Street Journal*, p. B1, at http://online.wsj.com/article/SB118487371421671957.html, July 20.
Fremlin, Grace Park. (2008). "Careful Contracts Reduce Risk," *China Business Review*, Vol. 35, January-February, pp. 34-39.
Fujimoto, Michelle, Laurel Harbour, Greta McMorris & Erin Sparkuhl. (2008). "Importing Products: Risks and Defense Strategies," *Defense Counsel Journal*, Vol. 75, pp. 238-242.
Gervang, Jim. (2007). "The China Question," *Business Finance*, at http://www.businessfinancemag.com/article/china-questia-1001, October 1.
Greene, Stephanie M. (2008). "Protecting Well-Known Marks in China: Challenges for Foreign Mark Holders," *American Business Law Journal*, Vol. 45, p. 371-398.
Haft, Jeremy. (2007). "The China Syndrome," *Wall Street Journal*, July 16, p. A12.
Lenckus, Dave. (2007). "China recall crisis underscores risk," *Business Insurance*, Vol. 41, at http://www.highbeam.com/doc/1G1-167710054.html, August.
Martin, Andrew & Griff Palmer. (2007). "China not sole source of dubious food," *New York Times*, p. C1, at www.nytimes.com/2007/07/12/business/12imports.html, July 12.
McIntyre, Doug A. (2009). "China Export Drop Signals Deepening U.S. Recession," at http://247wallst.com/2009/02/11, February 11.
Park, James. (2007). "Wal-Mart's China Imports Cost Nearly 200,000 U.S. Jobs," at http://blog.aflcio.org/2007/06/27/wal-marts-china-imports-cost-200000-us-jobs/html, June 27.
Quittner, Jeremy. (2007). "The China Code," *Business Week*, at www.businessweek.com/smallbiz/content/aug2007/sb2007089_716295.htm, August 17.
Sloma-Williams, Thomas A. (2007). "Helping China's Quality," *Quality Magazine*, Vol. 46, at http://www.qualitymag.com/article/column/BNP.
Smethurst, Ryan S. (2008). "The High Cost of Low Prices," *Risk Management*, Vol. 55, April, pp. 20-21.
Waldmeir, Patti. (2007). "Made in China but sued in America," at http://:us.ft.com/ftgateway/superpage.ft?news_id=fto07312007141832718l, July 31.
Walmart Watch. (2005). "Wal-Mart China: Cozy Multi-Billion Dollar Bedfellows," at http://walmartwatch.com/press/resleases/wal_mart_china_cocy_multi_billion-dollar-bedfellows.http, July 11.
Wilson, Lindsay. (2003). "Investors Beware: The WTO Will Not Cure All Ills in China," *2003 Columbia Business Law Review*, pp. 1007-1028.
Woellert, Lorraine. (2007). "Made in China. Sued Here," *Business Week*, p. 9, at www.indianalawblog.com/archives/2007/07/law_recovering.html, July.
Wong, Edward. (2008). "Courts Compound Pain of China's Tainted Milk," *New York Times*, October 17, p. A1.
Yi, Wu. (2007). "China Stands for Quality," *Wall Street Journal*, December 11, p. A27.

CHAPTER 4

Armentano, Dominick T. (1990). *Antitrust and Monopoly: Anatomy of a Policy Failure* (Holmes and Meier, 2d ed.).
Armentano, Dominick T. (1986). *Antitrust Policy: The Case for Repeal* (Cato Institute).
Bastiat, Frederic. (1968). *The Law* (Foundation for Economic Education).
Bergsten, Fred. (2009). "Obama needs to be bold on trade." *The Financial Times*, June 24, p. 11.
Boltuck, Richard and Robert E. Litan. (Eds.). (1991). *Down in the Dumps: Administration of the Unfair Trade Laws* (Brookings Institution).
Bovard, James. (1991). *The Fair Trade Fraud* (St. Martin's Press).
Bown, Chad P. (2007). "Global Antidumping Database 3.0," June (Brandeis University and Development Research Group), at http://people.brandeis.edu/~cbown/global_ad/.
Bown, Chad P. (2010). "Global Antidumping Database," at http://people.brandeis.edu/~cbown/global_ad/, March.
Cobb, Joe. (1994). *A Guide to the New GATT Agreement, Heritage Foundation Backgrounder,* No. 985, May 5.
Curtis, Philip J. (1994). *The Fall of the U.S. Consumer Electronics Industry: An American Trade Tragedy* (Quorum Books).
Curtiss, W.M. (1953). *The Tariff Idea* (Foundation for Economic Education).
Dale, Richard. (1980). *Anti-dumping Law in a Liberal Trade Order* (St. Martin's Press).
Dolan, Edwin G. & David E. Lindsey. (1994). *Economics* (Harcourt Brace College Publishers, 7th ed.).
Feinberg, Robert M. & Kara M. Reynolds. (2006). "The Spread of Antidumping Regimes and the Role of Retaliation in Filings." *Southern Economic Journal*, Vol. 72, No. 4, pp. 877-890.
Financial Times. (2009). "Anti-anti-dumping" [Editorial], November 20, p. 8.
Finger, J.M. (1991). "The Meaning of 'Unfair' in U.S. Import Policy," World Bank Working Paper, WPS 745, July.
Horlick, Gary N. (1993). "How the GATT Became Protectionist." *Journal of World Trade*, Vol. 27, October, pp. 5-17.
Jallab, Mustapha Sadni & James B. Kobak, Jr. (2006). "Antidumping as Anticompetitive Practice Evidence from the United States and the European Union," *Journal of Industry, Competition and Trade*, Vol. 6. pp. 253-275.
Jouvenel, Bertrand de. (1952). *The Ethics of Redistribution* (Cambridge University Press).
Kamarck, Lynn. (1994). "Uruguay Round Agreement Makes Substantial Changes To Antidumping Code," *East Asian Executive Reports*, No. 16, pp. 6, 15 -18, March.
Kenen, Peter B. (1994). *The International Economy* (Cambridge University Press, 3d ed.).
Knoll, Michael S. (1987). "United States Antidumping Law: The Case for Reconsideration," *Texas International Law Journal*, Vol. 22, pp. 265-290.
Koller, Ronald H. (1971). "The Myth of Predatory Pricing: An Empirical Study," *Antitrust Law and Economics Review*, Vol. 4, Summer, pp. 105-123.

Locke, John. (1986). *The Second Treatise on Civil Government* (Prometheus Books).
Malhotra, Nisha. (2006). "Is Antidumping Legislation a Threat to Competition? A Case Study of the U.S. Chemical Industry," *Competitiveness Review,* Vol. 16, No. 1, pp. 51-56.
McGee, John S. (1958). "Predatory Price Cutting: The Standard Oil (N.J.) Case," *Journal of Law and Economics*, Vol. 1, October, pp. 137-169.
McGee, Robert W. (1994). *A Trade Policy for Free Societies: The Case Against Protectionism,* (Quorum Books).
McGee, Robert W. (1993). "The Case to Repeal the Antidumping Laws," *Northwestern Journal of International Law & Business,* Vol. 13, pp. 491-562.
McGee, Robert W. (1991). "When Is Pricing Predatory," *Journal of Pricing Management*, Vol. 2, No. 2, pp. 40-43.
McGee, Robert W. & Yeomin Yoon. (2009). "Antidumping rules should be consigned to the history books," *The Financial Times* [Letter to the Editor], July 3, p. 8.
Messerlin, Patrick A. (1990). "Antidumping," in Jeffrey J. Schott (Ed.), *Completing the Uruguay Round: A Results-Oriented Approach to the GATT Trade Negotiations* (Institute for International Economics), pp. 108-129.
Moore, Michael O. (2007). "Antidumping Reform in the WTO: A Pessimistic Appraisal," *Pacific Economic Review*, Vol. 12, No. 3, pp. 357-379.
Nivola, Pietro S. (1993). *Regulating Unfair Trade* (Brookings Institution).
Nozick, Robert. (1974). *Anarchy, State, and Utopia* (Basic Books).
Palmeter, David. (1995). *United States Implementation of the Uruguay Round Antidumping Code* (unpublished manuscript on file with authors).
Salvatore, Dominick. (1993). "Trade Protectionism and Welfare in the United States," in Dominick Salvatore (ed.), *Protectionism and World Welfare* (Cambridge University Press), pp. 311-335.
Schott, Jeffrey J. (1994). *The Uruguay Round: An Assessment* (Institute for International Economics).
United States General Accounting Office. (1994). "The General Agreement on Tariffs and Trade: Uruguay Round Final Act Should Produce Overall U.S. Economic Gains," Vol. 2, July, GAO/GGD-94-83b.
Vandenbussche, Hylka & Maurizio Zanardi. (2008). "What Explains the Proliferation of Antidumping Laws?" *Economic Policy*, Vol. 23, No. 53, pp. 93-138.
Wall Street Journal. (1994). "The Uruguay Round's Key Results," p. A6, December 15.

CHAPTER 5

Bello, Judith H. & Alan F. Holmer. (1994). "The North American Free Trade Agreement: Its Major Provisions, Economic Benefits, and Overarching Implications," in *The North American Free Trade Agreement: A New Frontier in International Trade and Investments in the Americas* (Judith H. Bello et al., eds., 1994).
Baz, Aureliano Gonzales. (2008). "Manufacturing in Mexico: The Mexican In-Bond (Maquila) Program," at http://www.bancomext-mtl.com/invest/vox128/htm.

Bhala, Raj. (2000). *International Trade Law: Theory and Practice* (Lexis-Nexis, 2d ed.).
Burtless, Gary et. al. (1999). *Globaphobia: Confronting Fears About Open Trade* (Brookings Institution).
Charnovitz, Steve. (1994). "The NAFTA Environmental Side Agreement: Implications for Environmental Cooperation, Trade Policy, and American Treaty Making," *Temple International and Comparative Law Journal*, Vol. 8, pp. 257-314.
Commission for Environmental Cooperation. (2008). "Trade in Environmentally Preferable Goods and Services," at http://www.cec.org/programs_projects/trade_environ_econ/project/index.cfm?projectID=13&varlan=English.
Convention on Biological Diversity. (1992).
Convention on International Trade in Endangered Species of Flora and Fauna. (1973).
Dicken, Peter. (2003). *Global Shift: Reshaping the Global Economic May in the 21st Century* (Sage Publications, 5th ed.).
Footer, Mary E. (1995). "The International Regulation of Trade in Services Following Completion of the Uruguay Round," *International Law*, Vol. 29, p. 453-481.
Gilpin, Robert. (1987). *The Political Economy of International Relations* (Princeton University Press).
House of Representatives. (1994). "Uruguay Round Trade Agreement, Statement of Administrative Action, Agreement Establishing the World Trade Organization," H.R. Doc. No. 316, 103d Cong., 2d Sess., Vol. 1, pp. 659-667.
House of Representatives. (1994). "Uruguay Round Trade Agreement, Statement of Administrative Action, Agreement on Technical Barriers to Trade," H.R. Doc. No. 316, 103d Cong., 2d Sess., Vol. 1, pp. 776-789.
Huang, Haixiao & Walter C. Labys. (2002). "Environment and Trade: A Review of Issues and Methods," *International Journal of Global Environmental Issues*, Vol. 2, at http://www.rri.wvu.edu/pdffilesd/labys2001-1.pdf.
Krugman, Paul. (1994). "Empirical Evidence of the New Trade Theories: The Current State of Play" [Conference paper presented], in *New Trade Theories: A Look at the Empirical Evidence* (Center for Economic Policy Research, Bocconi University, Milan ed.), at http://cepr.org/PUBS/BULLETIN/meets/291.htm.
Kubasek, Nancy & Gary S. Silverman. (2008). *Environmental Law* (Prentice Hall, 2d ed.).
Kyoto Protocol to the United Nations Framework Convention on Climate Change. (1997).
Mc McLarty, Taunya L. (1998). "Liberalized Telecommunications Trade in the WTO: Implications for the Universal Service Policy," *Federal Communications Law Journal*, Vol. 51, pp. 20-58.
McGee, Robert. (1994). *A Trade Policy for Free Societies* (Praeger).
Mugerwa, Nkambo. (1968). "Subjects of International Law," in *Manual of Public International Law* (Max Sorensen, ed.) (Macmillan), Chapter 5, p. 247-310.
Ohmae, Kenichi. (2005). *The Next Global Stage: The Challenges and Opportunities in Our Borderless World* (Wharton School Publications).
Sohn, Louis. (1973). "The Stockholm Declaration on the Human Environment," *Harvard Journal of Environmental Law*, Vol. 14, pp. 423 ff.
Suranovic, Steven. (2002). *International Labour and Environmental Standards*

Agreements: Is This Fair Trade? (Blackwell).
Union Label & Service Trades Department (2008). "Bill Would Axe NAFTA," at http://www.unionlabel.org/index.cfm, March/April.
United Nations Framework Convention on Climate Change, art. 2. (1992). S. Treaty Doc. No. 102-38, U.N.T.S Vol. 1771.
United Nations Environmental Programme. (1997). "Industrial Countries to Cut Greenhouse Gas Emissions by 5.2%" (Press Release), December 11.
U.S. International Trade Commission. (1997). "The Impact of the North American Free Trade Agreement on the U.S. Economy and Industries: A Three-Year Review," Pub. 3045, June.
U.S. International Trade Commission. (1998). "Global Assessment of Standards Barriers to Trade in the Information Technology Industry," Pub. No. 3141, November.
World Bank. (2008). "Country Classifications," at http://web.worldbank.org.
World Trade Organization. (2008). "Trade and Development," at http://www.wto.org/english/tratop_e/envir_e.htm.
World Trade Organization. (2008). "Doha Round," at http://www.wto.org/english/tratop_e/envir_e.htm.
World Trade Organization. (2009). "Doha Development Agenda: Negotiations, implementation and development," at http://www.wto.org/english/tratop_e/dda_e/dda-e.htm.
World Trade Organization. (2009). "Understanding the WTO: Settling Disputes," at http://www.wto.org/english/thewto_e/whatis_e/tif_e/disp1_e.htm

CHAPTER 6

Chao, Loretta. (2009). "U.S. urges China to revoke PC software rule; Beijing's order to pre-install Web filters on computers set to take effect on July 1[2009]," GLOBE AND MAIL (Toronto), June 25, 2009, at B11.
Choney, Suzanne. (2010). "iPad 3G Owners' E-Mail Addresses Hacked," June 9, 2010, at http://www.msnbc.msn.com/id/37602751/ns/technology_and_science-tech_and_gadgets/ (last visited July 22, 2010).
"Dammed if you do," ECONOMIST, June 27, 2009, at 49.
Donadio, Rachel. (2010). "Larger Threat Is Seen in Google Case," N.Y. TIMES, February 25, 2010 at A1, at http://www.nytimes.com/2010/02/25/technology/companies/25google.html?scp=1&sq=google%20executives%20convicted%20in%20italy&st=Search.
"Google: one million servers and counting,"*Pandia Search Engine News*, July 2, 2007, at http://www.pandia.com/sew/481-gartner.html (last visited July 18, 2010).
Hansell, Saul. (2009). "U.S. asks China to rescind edict requiring Web filters," INTERNATIONAL HERALD TRIBUNE, June 24, 2009, at A6, at http://www.nytimes.com/2009/06/25/world/asia/25censor.html.
Helft, Miguel. (2010). "Anger Leads To Apology From Google About Buzz," N. Y. TIMES. Feb 15, 2010, p. B.3.
Hester, Tom. (2008). "NJ justices call e-privacy surfers' right." STAR LEDGER April 22, 2008 Front Cover.

Hooper, John. (2010). "Google executives convicted in Italy over abuse video," THE GUARDIAN, February 24, 2010, at http://www.guardian.co.uk/technology/2010/feb/24/google-video-italy-privacy-convictions.

Indiviglio, Daniel. (2010). "A cowardly decision," USA TODAY. Jan 15, 2010. pg. A.12.

Interbrand (2009), "Best Global Brands 2009," at http://www.interbrand.com/best_global_brands.aspx (last visited July 19, 2010).

Internet Traffic Report, at http://www.internettrafficreport.com/ (last visited July 15, 2010).

Internet World Statistics, "Top 20 Countries with Highest Number of Internet Users," at http://www.internetworldstats.com/top20.htm (last visited July 15, 2010).

Internet World Statistics, "Top 58 Countries with the Highest Internet Penetration Rate," at http://www.internetworldstats.com/top25.htm (last visited July 15, 2010).

Lindler, Mark. (2010)."Is the iPad a consumption only device?" at http://marklindner.info/blog/2010/03/28/is-the-ipad-a-consumption-only-device/ (last visited July 21, 2010).

Lohr, Steve. (2010). "Privacy Concerns Limit Online Ads," http://bits.blogs.nytimes.com/2010/04/30/privacy-concerns-limit-online-ads-study-says/ (last visited July 21, 2010).

Markoff, John. (2009). "Internet's Anonymity Makes Cyberattack Hard to Trace," N.Y. TIMES, July 17, 2009 at A5, at http://www.nytimes.com/2009/07/17/technology/17cyber.html?scp=1&sq=Cyberattacks%20Jam%20Government%20and%20Commercial%20Web%20Sites%20in&st=Search

Markoff, John. (2010). "At Internet Conference, Signs of Agreement Appear Between U.S. and Russia," N.Y. TIMES, April 16, 2010 at A14, at http://www.nytimes.com/2010/04/16/science/16cyber.html?scp=5&sq=cyberterrorism&st=cse.

Markoff, John. & Andrew E. Kramer. (2009). "U.S. and Russia Differ on a Treaty for Cyberspace," N.Y. TIMES, June 28, 2009 at A1, at http://www.nytimes.com/2009/06/28/world/28cyber.html?_r=1&scp=1&sq=russia%20and%20internet&st=cse.

Markoff. John & Andrew E. Kramer. (2009). "In Shift, U.S. Talks to Russia on Internet Security," N.Y. TIMES, December 13, 2009, at http://www.nytimes.com/2009/12/13/science/13cyber.html?_r=1&scp=1&sq=Russia%20and%20cyberterrorism&st=cse.

"New Cisco Visual Networking Index Forecasts Global IP Traffic to Increase Fivefold by 2013," http://newsroom.cisco.com/dlls/2009/prod_060909.html (last visited July 15, 2010).

Nielsen Online Global Index Chart, at http://www.nielsen-online.com/resources.jsp?section=pr_netv (last visited July 15, 2010).

Norris, Floyd. (2010). "France Calls Google a Monopoly," N.Y. TIMES, July 2, 2010 at B1, at http://www.nytimes.com/2010/07/02/business/02norris.html?emc=eta1.

Privacy Rights Clearinghouse. "Privacy in Cyyberspace, at

http://www.privacyrights.org/fs/fs18-cyb.htm#Marketing (Last visited July 15, 2010).

Sang-Hun, Cho & John Markoff. (2009). "Cyberattacks Jam Government and Commercial Web Sites in U.S. and South Korea," N.Y. TIMES, July 9, 2009 at A4, at http://www.nytimes.com/2009/07/09/technology/09cyber.html?scp=2&sq=Cyberattacks%20Jam%20Government%20and%20Commercial%20Web%20Sites%20in&st=Search

Sylvers, Eric. (2009). "Prosecutors Press Case Against Google in Italy," N.Y. TIMES, at http://www.nytimes.com/2009/11/26/technology/companies/26video.html?scp=1&sq=Google%20and%20Italy&st=Search .

Tran, Tini. (2010). "China renews Google's operating license," ASSOCIATED PRESS, July 11, 2010, at http://www.google.com/hostednews/ap/article/ALeqM5gKrY51vO2V86xiICf35Q05J0FIEAD9GSQSR00 (last visited July 19, 2010).

Underwood, Lee. (2004), "A Brief History of Search Engines," at http://www.webreference.com/authoring/search_history/ (last visited July 15, 2010).

Made in United States
Troutdale, OR
11/03/2026

56847577R00055